THEORY FOR THE WORKING SOCIOLOGIST

THEORY FOR THE WORKING SOCIOLOGIST

FABIO ROJAS

Columbia University Press   *New York*

Columbia University Press
Publishers Since 1893
New York   Chichester, West Sussex
cup.columbia.edu
Copyright © 2017 Columbia University Press
All rights reserved

Library of Congress Cataloging-in-Publication Data
Names: Rojas, Fabio, 1972- author.
Title: Theory for the working sociologist / Fabio Guillermo Rojas.
Description: New York : Columbia University Press, [2017] |
Includes bibliographical references and index.
Identifiers: LCCN 2016032435 | ISBN 9780231181648 (cloth :
alk. paper) | ISBN 9780231181655 (pbk. : alk. paper) |
ISBN 9780231543699 (e-book)
Subjects: LCSH: Sociology. | Sociology—Research.
Classification: LCC HM585 .R65 2017 | DDC 301.072—dc23
LC record available at https://lccn.loc.gov/2016032435

Columbia University Press books are printed on permanent
and durable acid-free paper.
Printed in the United States of America

Cover design: Rebecca Lown

To Eric, a pitcher who can start and close games

CONTENTS

PREFACE

WHAT is the point of sociology? At the very least, a science of society should report facts. Sociology can tell us things, such as how many people there are, how much money people make, and how often they have children. But a science that *only* reports facts isn't really a science. It's more like a dictionary, useful for knowing specific words but not enough for understanding how language really works. We instead ask that science perform two additional tasks. First, when presented with facts, we ask that science provide explanations. If a sociologist tells us that "divorce is on the rise," he or she should also provide an explanation. What is causing people to divorce more often? Is it that people are more likely to get into bad marriages? Or have laws governing marriage changed? Second, sociologists should provide explanations that have some consistency or commonality. If a sociologist explains rising divorce rates in America by focusing on the law, he or she should ask if the law has a similar effect in France. Even more importantly, explanations should be consistent not only between contexts (America versus France) but also across different social processes. We don't want a "theory of marriage" to be completely different from the "theory of divorce."

The difference between a casual and a serious student of sociology is that the casual student is more interested in specific facts or explanations, whereas the serious student demands broader themes or ideas. The latter is analogous to how serious life scientists approach their subject matter. Sometimes, a biologist will look at a specific animal and ask about it—Why is a butterfly so colorful? Usually, though, they are interested in a broader idea—how natural selection encourages animals to have a specific appearance, such as colorful wings or shaggy fur. Even though the theory of natural selection must be carefully applied to organisms as varied as dogs and butterflies, most biologists recognize that the same principals apply to each case. Just as biologists want their science to have common themes, sociologists also seek broader behavioral explanations, and that is what defines modern sociology.

The purpose of this book is to explain the major ideas that motivate sociological research. I want to help the reader understand that sociology isn't just about specific facts (e.g., divorce rates); it is ultimately about general principles. I want to do this in a way that is accessible to undergraduates, early-career graduate students, and scholars in related fields who have an interest in what sociology has to offer. Thus, my strategy is to focus on four major themes that recur in modern sociological writings: inequality, decisions and resources, social structure and values, and social constructions.

Another part of my strategy is to present sociological research on specific topics that motivate or exemplify these ideas. For that reason, the book is filled with discussions of topics such as school segregation, bank runs, and political change. A study in one of these areas often produces an idea that contributes to broader discussions about general sociological theory. Another benefit of incorporating examples of empirical research is that the reader can clearly see the nuts and bolts of a sociological explanation.

Sociologists call such detailed explanations "mechanisms." This book discusses mechanisms a great deal in its attempt to clarify the link between classic texts, "grand" theory, and daily research. Thus, I hope that seasoned sociologists will find this book interesting because it highlights the often invisible links between theory and current research.

Now that I have explained what this book is trying to do, I can turn to the question of how it fits in the broader sociological landscape. It is inspired by earlier books that review sociological theory, but it tries to address shortcomings in these other works. For example, it is common for writers to present sociological theory through the works of classic authors, such as Max Weber and Émile Durkheim. In this approach, social theory becomes the story of a few seminal thinkers.[1] This "Great Man" approach to sociology is structured like a Western civilization course organized around the "greatest events" in its history. Students spend their time reading original texts and commentaries.[2]

There is merit in this approach to theory. It is accessible: Karl Marx is easier to understand than Marxism. Most people will relate better to a person than to an abstract claim about social behavior. The Great Man approach has other strengths. By reading social theory as a discussion among leading figures, a student can readily see the underlying continuity of social thought. Great Man sociology connects the sociological discipline to the broader currents of Western thought. For example, sociology emerged from earlier forms of thought, such as history and political economy. Classical sociologists, such as Weber, straddled older intellectual traditions as they formulated the principal questions for modern sociology.

Although extremely valuable, the Great Man presentation of social theory has drawbacks. It focuses too much on individual authors, so a student can easily forget that their writings embody a theoretical commitment that must be excavated and examined. It also obscures the fact that classical authors remain important because they formulated theories that continue to be tested and evaluated in modern research. Focusing on the Great Men of sociology encourages drift between theory and practice. After tirelessly forging through Weber's *Protestant Ethic and the Spirit of Capitalism* ([1905] 1958), many students find it hard to make the connection to modern discussions of Protestant religion and contemporary theories of culture. They focus on *Weber's* ideas rather than on a more generic theory of action that now motivates multiple areas of research such as cultural sociology, historical sociology, and organizational analysis.

The separation of classical sociology and contemporary practice is a real problem. Michael Lounsboury and Ed Carberry, two sociologists who work in the field of organizational behavior, reviewed articles in leading organizational studies journals to understand how scholars discussed Weber's ideas about bureaucracy.[3] They found that Weber was frequently cited but that his ideas were rarely used or properly employed. Citations of Weber were ritualistic rather than informative. Weber was cited because scholars think they have to cite Weber! Journal article authors may have mentioned classical social theory because they felt an obligation to do so, not because they were seriously interested in engaging with these ideas. I suspect that the ritualistic citation of classical social theory continues in other areas of sociology as well. Researchers probably feel that immersing oneself in the classics is best left for scholars who specialize in "social theory," which in their minds often means opaque and complex books written decades, if not centuries, ago.

A second frequently encountered approach to social theory is topical, which means that the authors review the ideas of sociology as they emerge from the study of specific social processes, such as racial attitudes or consumer behavior. Many textbooks adopt this approach. Social theory, in this view, is the accumulation of insights obtained through the study of sociology's empirical foci.[4] This approach, too, has much to recommend it. As sociologists introduce new topics through research, they become part of the theoretical canon. The topical-survey approach to social theory highlights the depth of sociological thought. Sociological theory is a rare discipline in that its tools can be applied to topics as varied as voting, language, firm behavior, and racial discrimination.

The topical approach to sociology can be criticized as well, however. It recognizes the diversity of sociology, but its weakness is that it conflates topic and theory. It identifies a subject of interest with a general principle that implies an empirical regularity. But a topic, such as the link between social class and college attendance, can be analyzed with many different theories. When trying to explain why children of wealthy families attend college more often than children from poor families, sociologists may appeal to socialization (e.g., wealthy parents train their children to expect college) or cost–benefit calculations (e.g., the expected benefit of college attendance is less for low-income students).[5] The topic is education, but the theories explaining the topic are varied.

Nowhere is this conflation of topic and theory more evident than in the treatment of globalization. Social scientists have noted that the world's population is densely connected and that a global community of economic and political actors has emerged. For example, many, if not most, people are involved in a global economy. A car, for example, has thousands of parts that are manufactured in Mexico, China, and Vietnam. These parts may be shipped to a production facility in the American Midwest, and the final product may be sold in Europe. The world has seen the rise of a global culture promoted by a network of elites in business, politics, and the arts who travel among the world's largest cities. The rise of global society is so important that many social theory texts and anthologies now have sections dedicated specifically to globalization.[6] Although globalization is no doubt an extremely important topic, the inclusion of a "globalization theory" section in a theory book raises interesting questions. Do discussions of globalization require genuinely new theories? Or do globalization scholars use preexisting theory to shed light on an important new social development?

It is impossible to settle that question here, but I can give you examples of a sociologist who presents new theories to discuss globalization and another who uses preexisting theory. In her book *The Global City: New York, London, Tokyo* (1991), Saskia Sassen argues that a network of cities are closely linked together because they have become focal points of global capitalism. At the time Sassen published her book, she introduced a genuinely new concept to sociology—the "global city" that stands atop the world's economy because of its central position in networks of trade. In her discussion of global cities, she came to terms with the fact that improvements in transportation, communication, and business organization allow people in a few urban centers to quickly trade, interact, and compete with each other, even if they are thousands of miles away from each other. In the early 1990s, the "global city" was a new concept that contradicted earlier urban theorists who thought that cities were on the decline because people could communicate and work from remote locations.

Immanuel Wallerstein is another key figure in the study of globalization. He presented globalization as the outcome of capitalist forms of production in the West.[7] Firms need cheap labor and wish to work in an environment with lax regulation, so they establish manufacturing facilities in other countries.

This explanation applies ideas from Marxist social theory to the current situation. Globalization is merely class exploitation on a massive scale. Indeed, one can appreciate the appeal of Marxist theory because it can be used to describe various things, such as global trade, inequality within the United States, and social conflict from the time of the French Revolution.

Sassen's and Wallerstein's approaches to globalization share much in common, but what is important here is the fact that Wallerstein firmly rooted his account in preexisting theory (Marxism), whereas Sassen's account generated a need for new theory because it focused on a phenomena, the global city, that was not anticipated or accurately described in earlier work. This comparison suggests that one can present globalization as a topic that can be studied with existing theory or as a topic of such novelty that it requires new theory. In either case, there remains an important distinction between topic and theory that remains essential to any account of social theory. Although it is true that our theories, explicit or tacit, guide our choice of empirical cases, it is also true that multiple theories can be used to study a single empirical phenomenon, which suggests that one should recognize that empirical cases and social theories are related but distinct things.

A third standard way to present social theory is through a series of abstract concepts or social "laws." Talcott Parsons, a major figure of mid-twentieth-century sociology, did this with a series of books presenting his theory of structural functionalism. In his view, all social theories had to address the problem of social order, which is the need to explain how individuals with diverse interests create a stable community. His books presented social theory as a series of statements about the theoretical properties of social systems (e.g., societies have "integrative functions").[8] Other sociologists are content with an inductive approach to social theory that tries to extract general principles from various cases and commentaries. One of sociology's earliest textbooks, *Introduction to the Science of Sociology* (1921) by Robert Park and Ernest Burgess, took this approach. Park and Burgess selected a series of readings from economics, law, and related areas. Parsons and his collaborators produced a similar book titled *Theories of Society* (1965). Starting with a synthetic essay by Parsons, *Theories of Society* presented a diverse set of readings ranging from Chicago school interactionism to H. L. A. Hart's legal theory.

Sociologists will sometimes discuss theory in the most general terms. The essence of this approach is to present the broadest and often most decontextualized version of social theory. The strategy is to interpret theoretical texts and then to explicate the underlying logic. A classic example is *Twenty Lectures: Sociological Theory Since World War II* (1987) by Jeffrey C. Alexander. Alexander presents a version of Parson's theory of order and defends it against criticisms levied in the 1970s and 1980s. The result of this exercise is an extensive presentation of structural functionalism and its antecedents. There is much value in such an exercise. Being abstract allows one to directly understand a particular case. "This is an example of system integration!" The social theory text, such as Alexander's, was also thoughtfully used by the theorists who came before Parsons.

There are drawbacks to this approach, however. By relying on theoretical statements, sociologists may forget the motivation for the theory or incorrectly apply it. They may spend more time on definitions and jargon than on actual research into the social world. This is precisely what happened to Parsons. Critics accused him of being wordy and opaque. According to them, Parsons was more interested in definitions than in actual social life.[9] Generations of sociology students were required to memorize Parsons's AGIL scheme without ever quite understanding how it relates to schools, communities, or other common sociological topics.[10] Perhaps the most notable drawback is that purely abstract presentations of sociology may overlook important empirical studies or even fail to adequately explain how one translates broad theory into the everyday task of sociology, which is to explain observed social behavior.

An alternative to Great Man sociology, topical surveys, and abstraction is a focus on social mechanisms. By "social mechanism," I mean an explanation of how some feature of the social world leads to or causes a future state of the social world.[11] The metaphor is mechanical and pragmatic. In a mechanism, different things move together, leading to an outcome.[12] Neil Gross suggests that mechanisms are ways of explaining what happens between cause and effect and that the explanation is at a "lower" level that uses less-complex units of analysis.[13] Those who present social theory in terms of mechanisms have some expectation that the explanation may be relevant to other cases, but they do not usually expect unqualified generalizability of the explanation, as do proponents of "social laws." This is not the only way one can talk about social mechanisms, but most discussions of mechanisms focus on the idea that some distinct action or process clearly leads to a second outcome in a causal fashion, and the argument is presented in enough detail so that a consideration of any earlier part of the explanation logically entails the next step of the argument. The sociologist can clearly see how these cause-and-effect chains represent themselves in actual social life.

For example, if I say that the financial crisis of 2008 caused the Occupy Wall Street movement of 2011, then one might reasonably ask, "How, exactly, do home foreclosures and job loss lead to a protest movement three years later?" A mechanism-based explanation would have to walk the reader through a number of steps explaining how rising unemployment, mortgage fore-closures, and other economic events motivated people to join the movement. The specifics of the explanation might vary. A psychology-oriented explanation might focus on how anger toward the financial system encouraged people to express their political views. An alternative explanation is that the crisis made it possible for political activists to attract more attention to their cause. In that perspective, people are always complaining about the government, but the foreclosure crisis suggested to activists that it was time to rally people around a new movement.

Thus, mechanism-based explanations for the Occupy move-ment may vary and might even contradict each other. Mecha-nisms may in some cases depict relatively linear cause-and-effect relations but in others involve more subtle arguments about feedback loops of cause and effect. But they all share two things: cause-and-effect chains and logically sufficient detail. With this approach, you always need a "nuts and bolts" explanation of how you get from point A to point B.

The idea of a mechanism can be very important for under-standing the underlying structure of sociological thought. The mechanisms that appear in a variety of sociological accounts reveal shared theoretical commitments. The sociologist who rejects social values as an explanatory variable and instead focuses on exploitation is probably drawing on the models that Marxists use. Marxists, in turn, offer mechanisms that share many simi-larities with critical race theorists and feminist sociologists. Not surprisingly, a number of writers have argued that these varied traditions rest on a shared theoretical foundation.[14]

Thus, mechanisms offer an additional way to conceptualize the overarching structure of sociological thought. Rather than focusing on canonical texts, one might approach theory in a more inductive manner, starting with well-known and influential examples of sociology, and inquire about shared mechanisms. What mechanisms are described? When can mechanisms be grouped together because they rely on similar logic, even if the empirical cases appear different? Similar mechanisms suggest the translation of a more general intuition about social life into multiple specific situations.

Mechanism-oriented sociology is not immune to criticism. Some sociologists believe that the concept of mechanism is poorly defined, and others note that it is difficult to establish that a variable affects an outcome via causation. Nevertheless, the concept of mechanism closely resembles what sociologists do in their daily research. Perhaps it is the best description of what a satisfactory sociological explanation must accomplish: plausibly connect different observations of the social world into a logical chain of cause and effects.[15]

Mechanisms have great value for a book about sociological theory. They are constructed by arguing for a clear link between social causes and social outcomes, which means that they often have a foundation in empirical research. Sociological research often hinges on a claim that some factor, such as social class, affects some social outcome, such as education. Even when the research provides overwhelming evidence for a correlation in this example, there remains the question, "How exactly does a child's social class actually result in lower rates of college attendance?" The response to this question requires that the researcher translate his or her theory into a more concrete story of how family wealth affects a child's ability to compete in school.

Therefore, mechanism-based sociology provides a much-needed link between social theory and contemporary empirical work. For many sociologists, "social theory" appears removed from their daily practice. They don't feel that extended presentations of abstract theories can guide their research or that close readings of classic texts will help them resolve empirical puzzles. Mechanisms show how theory is ever present in sociology because research must always confront the question of converting abstract principles into believable chains of cause and effect. If empirical research is to provide a coherent account of the social world, the mechanisms generated through research must employ the same language and provide compatible answers. The alternative—having mechanisms based on different ideas, utilizing different languages, and yielding inconsistent answers— produces social research that is ad hoc and contradictory. Thus, mechanism-oriented sociology has the promise of allowing sociologists not just to recognize regularities between empirical cases but also, if they make the effort to absorb the lessons of the field, to recognize commonalities among explanations and thus to map the terrain of the discipline.

What should a book motivated by mechanisms look like? First, the book should speak to sociological practice, not to history of social thought or nuanced close readings of classic texts. A book inspired by mechanisms should ask, "Why is *this* research so resonant? What does that resonance tell us about the way sociologists see the world?" In other words, it should show the connections between the practice of sociologists and the longstanding concerns of the classical theorists and their contemporary descendants. It should use cutting-edge modern sociology as an opportunity to explore how empirical arguments rely on and generate developments in social theories.

Second, such a book should bluntly recognize that sociology has not converged on common ground. Rather than force a single theoretical framework upon a diverse field, the book should accept sociology's competing frameworks and how they generate divergent mechanisms. Sociology is not a chaotic Tower of Babel, as critics charge,[16] but, rather, the field has multiple starting points that reflect different priorities. Any description of the different theoretical frameworks and their underlying assumptions has to take into account the motivations for these frameworks and various strategies of explanation.

Third, the book should express skepticism toward claims of novelty among sociological theories. Although proponents of a particular theory may claim that their theory is new or completely incompatible with rivals, this is rarely the case. Theories often incorporate ideas and tools from earlier generations of social thought. There is also substantial cross-over as scholars play "arbitrage" and create new insights by linking previously disconnected theory. Theory spillover is evident when one examines the mechanisms offered by empirical researchers. Furthermore, when theories are applied to social life, they require modification or extension because models have their limits. To produce a plausible cause-and-effect chain, a researcher may have to combine new and old ideas or borrow from other styles of argument. This qualification suggests that a theory book should avoid presenting sociology as a sequence of completely new innovations. Sociological theory is instead more like a toolbox or playbook of ideas that are used in practice.

In the 1980s and 1990s, for example, Marxists began adopting the tools of strategic-action theory. They were confronted with the argument that worker revolutions present a theoretical problem: Why would the average worker bother to participate? Why don't all revolutionary worker movements collapse due to free riding? To resolve this problem, Marxists adopted the language of choice to discuss incentives.[17] Similarly, some sociologists of gender have found that arguments from human biology can address how men and women respond differently to their environment.[18] These two examples reveal the loose theoretical boundaries in sociology. To establish believable mechanisms, sociologists routinely integrate many types of arguments.

The overlap between theories motivates the need for synthetic work. It is important to survey various empirical findings and theoretical arguments in order to group them together by virtue of some overarching idea or concept. The fourth concern of the mechanism-oriented theory book is to discuss these grand syntheses and link active research agendas to more general arguments. By looking at how sociologists link different theoretical strands, one can see the emerging landscape of twenty-first-century sociology. Even though sociology doesn't employ a single language, one can see how new ideas emerge from points of contact between different schools of thought.

Each approach to social theory relies on an often unstated philosophy of knowledge, a belief about how knowledge is created. The historical approach to theory is based on a cumulative model of sociological thought. Seeing how Weber responded to Marx or how Durkheim responded to Herbert Spencer allows the sociologist to understand the intellectual and historical forces that shaped modern social theory.

The mechanism-based approach to social theory employs a different knowledge model that has an inherent element of puzzle solving. We are confronted with social trends, observations about people's behavior, and other data that require explanation. We then develop ad hoc explanations inspired by previous research and conjectures stemming from sociology's classic texts. From this point of view, knowledge isn't necessarily created by exploring a certain theorist's ideas, but we don't reject the classics, either. Rather, we focus on the point of contact between theories and empirical data. The sociologist produces chains of cause–effect relations that are subject to criticism and testing.

Once he or she has done this numerous times, he or she can try to articulate a more general principle that implies the various mechanisms. Alternatively, the sociologist can produce mechanisms by translating abstract theories into descriptions of cause–effect chains. Mechanisms derived from a theory can be used to judge the value of the theory.

In practice, mechanism-based theory and history-oriented theory appear to be quite different. A historical and often immersive approach to theory often produces a strong theoretical commitment. A vivid moment from my own life illustrates this point. As a graduate student, I was once invited to a faculty party for a visiting scholar who was being considered for an appointment at the university. When I arrived, one of my professors loudly proclaimed, "This is Fabio. He is an institutionalist!" As a person committed to institutional theory, while I was in graduate school at least, I naturally inclined toward explanations that rely on the idea that human beings are encumbered with all sorts of norms and rules that constrain their behavior. A commitment to a specific theoretical school has value. It provides guidance for research and a ready-to-go vocabulary for describing social behavior. It also has costs, though. An overly strong commitment to a single theory can hamper research.

In contrast, the mechanism-based approach focuses on sociologists' daily empirical practice. The translation of theoretical ideas into research agendas requires a link between the concepts that motivate theory (social class) and the specific things that can be measured (income or occupation). The practice of social research isn't what happens after you learn some theory. It is what motivates the theory, tests the theory, and is framed by the theory. Theories, cases, and evidence mutually create each other.

These comments belie my pragmatic philosophy of science. In my view, a priori theories of scientific practice are incomplete at best. No single method or approach can capture everything that social scientists need to do. This view was articulated by philosopher Paul Feyerabend, who famously argued that in science "anything goes."[19] I don't believe in the strongest version of this view. Carefully investigating every claim is impossible. Experience and reason can be used to create useful boundaries for practice. At the same time, there is a more sensible formulation of Feyerabend's view. Sociologists have limits to their knowledge and reason. The complexity of the social world may exceed the capacity of a theory to capture that complexity. Thus, there is justification to being pragmatic and experimental at times, even to entertain hunches whose logic or intuition may not be immediately obvious. Reaching a point of clarity might require some very messy intellectual work.

Mechanisms are one way to tap into that often chaotic process of knowledge creation. The sociologist who focuses on specific social processes will create opportunities for skepticism and intellectual experimentation. The often poor fit between theory and observation makes it possible to question theories and generate new ideas. For that reason, mechanism-oriented sociology is pragmatic; it is an intellectual practice that deserves its own version of social theory.

This book covers some familiar ground. For example, it occasionally discusses classic authors, such as Émile Durkheim and W. E. B. Du Bois. It also has some similarities to earlier books that focus on specific topics, such as education, because some topics seem to encourage the articulation of certain mechanisms and theories. It is likewise similar to books that survey emerging topics. I also use examples from contemporary sociology, such as globalization.

The differences lie in the book's organization and presentation of the materials. There is very little discussion of specific sociological writers or their times. I won't discuss Berlin in the time of Georg Simmel or Michel Foucault and the French intellectual scene of the 1960s. I won't discuss an empirical research topic solely because it is popular. Rather, I discuss empirical research because it exemplifies a style of argument or the specific author who presented a mechanism that embodies a classic or emerging theoretical concern. This book uses the language of mechanisms to illuminate the dialogue between long-standing or emerging theories and the practice of sociological research.

For this reason, the book does not offer distinctions that are sometimes found in other sociological theory books. For example, it is common for sociologists, especially in introductory texts, to discuss the differences between consensus and conflict theories. For me, the distinction between conflict and consensus is misleading because a theoretical framework can account for both conflict and consensus. The degree of conflict in society is a "dependent" variable, and theory provides the "independent" variable. Marxism once again is an excellent example. It is often labeled as a conflict theory because of its focus on class conflict.[20] However, Marxism also has a theory of ideology, which explains why people don't fight all the time and why there is sometimes widespread belief in the justice of a society where people are seemingly oppressed. Thus, the conflict/consensus distinction is not useful because Marxism predicts both conflict and consensus. It is instead better to present Marxism as a theory of domination where possession of resources entail social practices that in different circumstances might lead to either conflict or consensus. The mechanism involves the possession of resources, exclusive access to goods and social privilege, and a repertoire of actions and beliefs that allow people to maintain status. The opportunities and strategies that allow those who possess resources to attain and sustain status is the crux of Marxist explanations of inequality. These same mechanisms sometimes create opportunities for challenge. Exercising privilege may undermine the legitimacy of high-status groups, resulting in conflict.

My thumbnail description of Marxist theories is focused on mechanisms and makes it clear that other types of sociology rely on similar sorts of explanations. Feminist sociologists often provide analogous explanations of male domination that also focus on acquiring exclusive access to goods or establishing a superior position in social interactions.[21] Likewise, critical race sociologists explore the different ways that people of a certain racial or ethnic background claim status.[22] Instead of separating Marxism, feminism, or race theorists into different camps, I admit that they have commonalities and often share overlapping intellectual genealogies. Sociologists working in these diverse areas often present similar mechanisms because they adhere to an underlying model of society motivating particular types of explanations. Researchers assume that social life is defined by group divisions and that individuals do things, consciously or unconsciously, to preserve and exploit these divisions.

In addition to theories of power and domination, such as Marxism, this book describes three more strands of sociology. "Strategic action" refers to a type of sociology that heavily focuses on how individuals make decisions and pursue their goals. In a sense, this entire tradition of sociology stems from Weber's observation that social action can vary in its purpose. According to his classic description of social action, some actions are pursued for their own sake (value-rational action); others may satisfy an emotional need (affectual action); and yet others may be done out of habit (traditional action). For example, people might go to church because they believe it is intrinsically good, and they think little of the consequence of the time it requires, or church attendance satisfies a personal need to contact the divine.

Some attend church simply because that is what they have always done. In contrast, one might act in a certain way because it achieves a specific goal. One is very conscious of consequences and then considers the costs and benefits. Weber called this behavior "instrumental action" in that it is goal directed and the goal is not merely habit, affect, or perceived intrinsic moral value. The churchgoer might attend services because he or she wishes to meet an influential person or simply to show others that he or she is pious. If influential people do not attend the church or nobody notices one's participation, then the individual may consider church not worthy of his or her time. The character of instrumental action is the active decision-making involved and the weighing of costs and benefits.

After Weber, many attempts were made to provide a general description of how individuals make instrumental choices. I use the label *strategic action* because these attempts either try to describe the trade-offs and calculations that people make or describe the types of resources that people use in achieving their goals. The character of strategic-action theory is highly individualistic in that it focuses relentlessly on individual choices, often subordinating arguments about larger social structures or inequalities. Not surprisingly, strategic-action theories often draw from economics for their basic mechanisms. Mechanisms in this tradition often describe how incentives lead to specific behaviors. The sociological contribution to this tradition is to be found in the discussion of how people use their social relationships to advance their goals. Another important contribution is in the study of unintended consequences and "emergent processes" that happen when large groups of people interact while pursuing their own goals and inadvertently create new social structures.

I call a third strand of theory "values and social structures" because it is an attempt to connect what people think (values) to the social systems (structures) that they build. In this type of sociology, it is very common to speak of social values as a starting point. In America, for example, we value individual freedom. So one might ask how our social structures reflect our belief that individual freedom is good. For example, are schools designed to help students exercise their individual freedom? The answers vary. On the one hand, one might argue that the public directly influences schools because school boards are run by elected leaders. Thus, if voters think freedom is important, teachers will have to create a school that allows students to exercise their freedom. On the other hand, maybe schools don't enable a student's individual freedom. Once the school board meeting is over and the mission statement has been read, teachers retreat to their classrooms and teach as they please. Although these two arguments differ in their final answer, they use similar ingredients. Both describe how schools—a structure—respond to values. In general, I label social theory that focuses on values, social structures, and their interaction a "values and structures" theory.

The final type of sociology concerns the ways that people define their world. Often called "social constructionism," this type of social theory focuses on how people define what is real. Social constructionists focus on the fact that knowledge is learned and that people produce the norms that govern their behavior. The mechanisms that constructionists offer tend to focus on how individuals are influenced by others and how social conditions affect what people perceive to be real or legitimate.

After reviewing each of these four major strands of social theory and investigating the mechanisms and causal accounts they offer, I finish the book with a short chapter that shows how researchers expand the frontier of sociology by combining different types of social theory. Our understanding of the social world does not necessarily advance when we rigidly apply old formulas to new problems. Progress might happen when we juxtapose ideas and creatively blend theories. In that spirit, the concluding chapter of the book presents interesting examples of modern sociologists who cross intellectual boundaries in their work.

• • •

Now you know what this book is about: social theory in four steps, with a healthy dose of contemporary research and mechanisms. There remains the question of whether you in particular should read it. I have a few audiences in mind.

First, many readers among the general public are curious about what sociology has to offer. Perhaps academics in a related area, such as history and political science, want to know if sociological theory is relevant to their work. Each chapter has numerous examples that would be of interest to historians, political scientists, economists, and other social researchers. These examples motivate broader theories that define modern sociology. The text, then, should be very accessible to these readers.

Second, students will benefit from this book, especially advanced sociology undergraduates and graduate students who seek a road map that connects the diverse arguments found in the discipline. A more experienced sociologist can read an academic journal article and immediately grasp its logic of explanation. "This is clearly an institutionalist argument," or "This relies on Marxism and critical theory." These connections are often unclear to students, however. They do not see how broad theoretical positions are translated into arguments about schools, markets, or neighborhoods. The issue, in my view, is that many treatments of social theory focus on intellectual history and original texts. As noted earlier, these approaches are valuable, but students are left with the impression that social theory is an exercise in intellectual history and thus not relevant to current social analysis. By using contemporary work as a lens for thinking about theory and social explanation, they will see how classic ideas remain relevant and how new ideas are created to solve problems in older theories.

This book can be used in courses that survey social theory, either as a primary text or as a text that can supplement readings of original texts. It may be read by itself as an overview of how sociologists explain the world. Students can use this text as an introduction to the field to help guide their reading or at the end of a sequence of courses when they have the need for a text that provides some sort of synthesis. An instructor might also want to weave together classic readings and portions of this text. For example, a social theory course might include a section focusing on how sociologists explain inequality. In such a section, students would read chapter 2 of this book along with classic and contemporary writers such as Weber, Marx, Du Bois, Patricia Hill Collins, Eduardo Bonilla-Silva, and Annette Lareau.

This book might also help early-career graduate students who need to "catch up." Sociology is a field that attracts doctoral students with undergraduate degrees in the humanities, physical sciences, and social sciences as well as in sociology. There are also undergraduate sociology programs that are very applied in character and in which students take few, if any, courses that promote a more systematic understanding of the field. So it is not unusual for students starting their doctoral education to lack an overall understanding the types of arguments that appear in the field. I was one such student, and it would have been quite helpful to have something that quickly explained the kinds of arguments that my teachers were mentioning in the seminar room.

Third, empirically oriented sociologists may enjoy this book because it focuses on the dialogue between current research and theory. As sociologists generate new explanations for phenomena, they create mechanisms. The accumulation of mechanisms creates a demand for coherence. What explanation ties these mechanisms together? Due to specialization and time constraints, even a thoroughly engaged sociologist may not appreciate how social theory has evolved through the profession's collective work. Many researchers may not see the web of connections between research and theory development. An exploration of the back and forth between empirical research and theory fills an important gap in the literature on sociological theory.

Finally, this book is aimed at the reader who asks, "Where is it all going?" When one reads sociological work, as in any discipline, it is easy to get lost in the forest of empirical studies. It's hard to understand how studies of elementary schools and global human rights treaties might rely on the same type of argument or reflect an unstated theoretical mood, but they often do. It can also be hard to understand how sociological traditions can talk to each other. But, once again, they do. By uncovering the common explanations employed in a wide range of studies, this book will help the reader see the themes that run from classical social theory to the research that defines modern sociology.

ACKNOWLEDGMENTS

THIS book would not have been possible without encouragement and assistance from many people. I thank many careful student readers at Indiana University: Josh Coker, Joe DiGrazia, Rachel Green, Anne Groggel, Peter Lista, and Nik Summers. I thank my Indiana colleagues Pam Barnhouse Walters, Tim Hallett, Pamela Braboy Jackson, Scott Long, Eliza Pavalko, and Brian Steensland for providing ideas and discussion that shaped various sections of this book. I also thank earlier readers, who read a very different draft of the book or were consulted on various sections: Rene Almeling, Bryan Caplan, Trey Causey, Russell Funk, Robin Hanson, Fritz Harrison, Michael T. Heaney, Dan Hirschman, Omar Lizardo, Brooke Long, Marit Rehavi, Rachel Rinaldo, and Nick Rowland. Several readers pointed out errors and suggested improvements on the most recent draft: Syed Ali, Pierre Brunelle, Chris Eberhardt, Michael Gibson-Light, Jeff Guhin, Derin Kent, Wee Kiat Lim, Isaac Reed, Rodrigo Ignacio Rojas Zevallos, and Pedro Souza. I thank Megan Levinson, who read multiple versions. I thank Annie Barva, who copyedited this text, and the editorial and production staff at Columbia University Press. My profound gratitude also goes to six anonymous peer reviewers.

Enormous gratitude goes to Eric Schwartz at Columbia University Press, who encouraged the project and stayed with it. I also thank the Robert Wood Johnson Foundation, which provided financial support while I wrote the first draft. My family was very supportive: Elizabeth Pisares, Merlyn Rojas, and Coltrane Rojas, who was born between the first and second versions of the book. I thank the students in my graduate course on social organization and undergraduate course on social theory, who did not consent to being the "test subjects" for various ideas in this book. Finally, I thank all the sociologists whose research made this book possible. Without their courage and imagination, there would have been nothing to write about.

THEORY FOR THE WORKING SOCIOLOGIST

1

WHAT COUNTS AS SOCIAL THEORY
FOR THIS BOOK?

SHOW me a thousand Americans, and I'll show you a thousand "educational outcomes." Of these Americans, 871 completed high school, and 299 of these high school graduates earned a college degree.[1] Faced with these facts, most people would ask a rather obvious question: Why do some people complete college, but others struggle, often unsuccessfully, to earn a high school diploma? Many things might explain why a person completes college. A person with low intelligence will have a tough time completing school. Perhaps it's a matter of motivation. Some people just find it difficult to sit through algebra lectures.

Psychological factors such as cognitive ability and ambition matter a great deal, but sociologists have a special interest in social context. They want to know how a person's social environment affects his or her future. If a person has enough intelligence to perform schoolwork, how does his or her social environment enable or undermine the ability to succeed in school? Sociologists offer a number of answers. For example, it is thought that some parents, especially those who are already well educated or wealthy, help their children by reading to them. The intuition is that educated and wealthy parents are more likely or more able than poor parents to give their children the academic skills needed to succeed in school.[2] Other sociologists have argued that wealthier parents endow their children with "cultural capital"—the social resources, such as knowledge or personal style, that help achieve economic success. Children with high cultural capital, for example, might have more knowledge of French or art. These parents teach kids how to eat with the right fork, so to speak.[3]

Step back and ask what these two explanations have in common and what makes them sociological as opposed to psychological (e.g., high IQ leads to school success). The transmission of academic skills and cultural capital are tied to wealth and privilege. Privileged young people share a family environment that reflects "social class." The more general principle is straightforward. Well-off people enjoy high status within society, and they do their best to ensure that their children continue to enjoy the benefits of high status. These efforts may be conscious, via private schools, or they may be more indirect, such as encouraging children to speak the right way at public school. Social class isn't the only way that sociologists explain educational outcomes such as college completion, but it serves as a classic example of sociological argument: a certain group of people (the wealthy) mobilizes its resources (money, skills) to ensure a future outcome (children who continue to be wealthy).

Let's consider another example—poverty policy. It is very common for governments to provide financial support to low-income individuals. Observers normally view financial support for the poor to be a clear benefit, a political victory for the poor. However, Frances Fox Piven and Richard Cloward argue in *Regulating the Poor: The Functions of Public Welfare* (1971), a highly cited book on poverty policy, that public-welfare programs have placated the poor and reinforced their position. These outcomes often occurred unintentionally. Rules for receipt of cash benefits

often required that recipients do things that would make it difficult for them to climb out of poverty, such as not allowing women
to receive benefits if they reside with able-bodied men. Piven and
Cloward's bolder claim is that policy makers used public welfare
as a tool to build a new majority for the Democratic Party in the
1950s and 1960s. The argument, roughly speaking, is that blacks
who migrated from the South to the North's industrial centers
became a key voting block. They were brought into the Democratic Party with a series of poverty-relief programs, administered
by workers closely associated with that party.

Piven and Cloward's controversial thesis is often seen as a
fascinating example of class analysis. Poor people have an interest in programs that give them material benefits. They may also
have an interest in challenging the state and demanding more
wide-scale reform. Wealthier people have opposing interests.
Expanded social benefits and political reforms might be financed
by increased taxes on their income and the massive redistribu-
tion of their wealth. In Piven and Cloward's view, mobilizing a
few resources to produce modest benefits for the poor might be
enough to forestall a broader political challenge that might have
extensive political and economic consequences. My summary of
the argument highlights the fact that it relies on a logic similar
to that of the earlier argument about education—namely, that
people of a certain social class use their resources to pursue their
goals. In the case of American welfare policy, Piven and Cloward
argue that political and economic elites have a shared interest in
preventing political challenges and that poverty policy is one of
the tools they use to achieve that goal.

The point of this book is to show how sociologists create
wide-ranging explanations of social life. Theories of capitalism
and class are one such example. Sociologists use class analysis
to explain things as wildly divergent as school outcomes, global

politics, popular culture, and family structure. In fact, explanations that rely on social class and economic forces have such a long history in sociology that they are instantly recognizable and have their own names. Explanations that rely on the benefits of wealth and property ownership are often called "Marxist," after German revolutionary Karl Marx, who argued that economic forces heavily influence most aspects of social life. Marxist theories, which rely on economic conditions and social class divisions, are one example of a broader class of explanations that explain inequality in terms of intergroup conflict, the deployment of superior resources, and the interplay of race, gender, and social class. This book also discusses three other broader types of sociological explanations: those that focus on forward-looking thinking and strategic action; those that look at how social values lead to social structure; and those that look at how people collectively assign meaning and interpret the world. Before getting to these examples, let's look at what the term *theory* means in this book.

THEORY, THEORY, THEORY

These two examples, school outcomes and poverty policy, show that sociology, like any other discipline, has a need for theory. But what exactly is theory? In this book, I define *theory* as an idea or collection of ideas that provides some coherence or commonality among explanations within a given domain of thought. It is the root of the plant, so to speak. Thus, physical theory refers to the ideas that give physics some underlying structure, in the same way that a social theory allows people to develop overlapping and consistent explanations of topics as diverse as schooling and voting.

Academic fields do not always have well-developed theories. In fact, they vary a great deal in their ability to produce theories that are widely accepted by practitioners as a logical foundation for their research. For example, physics and biology have extremely successful underlying theories that most practitioners seem to accept. In physics, we have the ideas of Isaac Newton and James Clerk Maxwell that describe the everyday physical world of motion and energy, while Albert Einstein and Niels Bohr offered laws that describe extremely large and small objects. In biology, nearly all biologists accept some form of Charles Darwin's theory of evolution.

Physics and biology are unusual. In contrast, most fields of inquiry have not developed theories that are universally accepted. It is more typical for a number of approaches to compete for attention in an area of study. For example, much contemporary philosophy is "analytical philosophy," which views philosophy as a very linguistically precise discussion of narrowly defined concepts and topics.[4] That is, a philosopher should take an idea, such as "color," and then rigorously examine its definition and what it entails. The underlying theory of analytic philosophy relies on formal logic and a theory of language that can be used to justify and develop other philosophical arguments. Analytic philosophy may be dominant, but it has competitors. Perhaps the most famous is "continental philosophy," which stems from writers such as Immanuel Kant and G. F. W. Hegel, who were willing to consider broad questions and answer them in a language that is quite different from that used in analytic philosophy.[5]

It has been argued that theory is too difficult, misleading, or fruitless for some fields. Unifying theories are bound to fail. Scholars and scientists should instead stick to "what works." For example, in 1982 literary scholars Steven Knapp and Walter Benn Michaels published an article titled "Against Theory." Their goal was to explain that any attempt to "govern" literary interpretations rested on the fallacy that the meaning of text was easily linked to its author's intention. The validity of this argument is not important in the present context. What matters is that Knapp and Benn Michaels's article continues to have great appeal in literary analysis because it speaks to the belief that general theories of poetry and fiction aren't particularly useful. It's just too hard to come up with an all-encompassing scheme for literary interpretation that will be helpful when confronted with the full range of novels, poetry, and drama that literary critics try to read. Also, by the time Knapp and Benn Michaels's article was published, many literary scholars were tired of theories that seemed removed from texts, such as postmodernism, and of rigid theories that offered very narrow rules for how one should interpret a novel, such as the New Criticism of the 1950s. The result of the skepticism was a retreat into literary pragmatism, where judging texts is often historical and contingent rather than rule based.

The social sciences tend to live in between theory skepticism and the relative theoretical unity of physics and biology. Most of the social sciences have a few major schools of thought. Economics has the "neoclassical" framework, which is a conceptually simple, if mathematically sophisticated, theory of how people make optimal choices.[6] People have options, assign some subjective value to each option, and choose the option with the best value, weighted by the probability that the option will happen (i.e., less value is assigned to things that rarely happen, such as winning the lottery). In addition, choices are constrained by budgets and other factors. There are also competing theories, such as behavioral economics, which focuses on cognitive limits to decision making, and Austrian economics, which rejects neoclassical concepts such as market equilibrium (e.g., prices will settle and reflect supply and demand) and suggests a more dynamic and historical approach to markets.[7]

Sociology is a bit more diverse than economics, where a large majority of economists employ some version of neoclassical theory.

Sociology contains multiple schools of thought, such as Marxism and institutionalism, and no school of thought has come to dominate the field, even though many attempts have been made to establish an all-encompassing theory of society. These different theories touch on the types of things that sociologists like to study, such as conflict and social interaction.

WHAT COUNTS AS
SOCIOLOGICAL THEORY?

The long discussion of what counts as sociological theory goes back decades and touches on the many ways that sociologists use the term *theory*. In fact, one scholar has identified at least eight different ways that the word *theory* is used in modern sociology.[8] In this section, I explain what I mean by *theory* in the context of this book. First, sociological theory should be a language for studying what people do when they come together in groups. Thus, any sociological theory should provide a terminology for describing groups and how people relate to each other. The importance of theory as a language can't be overstated. Intellectual communities can't thrive if they don't have a shared vocabulary. There will be little progress when people can't talk to each other and can't work with each other. Research projects would proceed with little reference to others. Thus, the application of a sociological theory entails a translation of ideas and observation into a lingua franca. The Marxist, to continue with an earlier example, would try to understand a community as divided into social classes based on people's position within the economy. How do the upper classes maintain their position? How do they assert their influence? The language of Marxism makes social explanation possible in that tradition.

Second, sociological theory must lead to detailed and logically coherent accounts that move from cause to effect. Contemporary sociologists call the chains linking cause and effect "mechanisms."[9] Mechanisms, which in an earlier era were called "social processes," provide a description of the social world at a level of detail that is persuasive and open to logical criticism and possibly empirical testing. Sociological theories should provide guidance in the construction of these detailed accounts of social life. In that sense, theory is generative.

In this book, I employ Neil Gross's definition of the term *social mechanism*: "A social mechanism is a more or less general sequence or set of social events or processes analyzed at a lower level of complexity or aggregation by which—in certain circumstances—some cause X tends to bring about some effect in the realm of human social relations."[10] In other words, when a sociologist describes this chain of events from cause to effect, he is describing a chain where each link is simpler than the overall process. He is also describing a chain of events that when "added up" is larger or more complex than the sum of its parts. Gross deftly notes that the definition is agnostic with respect to some philosophical issues that plague social theory. For example, there is a longstanding debate in the social sciences about whether explanations of group behavior must be logically reducible to individual action. In some traditions, such as strategic-action sociology, all actions are made by individuals. In other traditions, such as Durkheimian sociology, groups act collectively in ways that are logically distinct from what individuals do. One can produce social mechanisms from both types of sociological theory. This book sidesteps that question. A mechanism is about any chain of events, not just about those that describe individual or group processes.

Without theories and mechanisms, sociology would be overrun by vague concepts that fail to produce satisfactory causal accounts.

For example, people who read classical texts such as *The Protestant Ethic and Spirit of Capitalism* ([1905] 1958) often come away with the erroneous view that Max Weber believed that "Protestantism causes capitalism." A closer reading of Weber's text reveals, however, that he never made any such claim. Weber made a claim about Calvinists in early-modern Europe. By the time Calvinism appeared in Europe, people had developed new attitudes toward work that were coupled with religion. This specific combination of religious belief and cultural change provided an unusually fertile environment for creating capitalist institutions. Weber would have rejected any sort of attempt at formulating a broad historical law and instead argued that social change, such as the emergence of modern capitalism, is the result of very specific historical processes. At the same time, he was not completely antitheoretical. He did not believe that the historical analysis of one time period is not relevant to other time periods. He obtained broader theoretical lessons from history by relying on explanations of motivation, identity, and action that examine how specific identities interact with specific legal and political environments. This approach is not unlike that used by the medical researcher, who recognizes that drugs don't work the same way in every person. There are broader theories of chemistry, but the way drugs affect a specific patient depends on his or her genetic makeup, body chemistry, and social environment.

This summary of Weber's text highlights the need for sociologists to pay attention to mechanisms and theory. The problem with the statement "Protestantism caused capitalism" is not only that it is an inaccurate summary of Weber's argument but also that it is vague as stated.[11] How does a set of beliefs about Jesus actually lead to a corporation? What needs to be done is to show how a belief system (religion) encourages people to act in ways that create new belief systems (capitalism). In other words, it doesn't make sense to say that a religion caused an economic institution. But it does make sense to say that people who belong to a certain religion behave in ways that make it easier to start firms and accumulate wealth, which then leads to new economic institutions.

Third, sociological theory should be able to cross empirical domains. It should be exportable from one context to another. Sociological theory should be ambitious in its claims and not focus exclusively on particular phenomena. Much in the same way that Newton's laws should be applicable to moving cars as well as to billiard balls, sociological theories should illuminate many things. The sociologist who tries to explain homelessness should come up with an insight that might illuminate less-severe forms of poverty as well as income inequality in general.

NOT QUITE MIDDLE-RANGE THEORY

Readers familiar with the history of sociology may think that I advocate middle-range theory. Promoted by Robert Merton in the mid–twentieth century, "middle-range theory" is the name given to social theory developed by considering particular topics: "theories that lie between the minor but necessary working hypotheses that evolve in abundance during day to day research and all inclusive systematic efforts to develop a unified theory that will explain all the observed uniformities of social behavior, social organization and social change."[12] For example, one might develop theories of social roles and reference groups. The theory of each "middle-range" topic would eventually be merged into a "network" of topics.

Merton's argument for middle-range theory has had wide appeal among sociologists. Those dedicated to a specific empirical issue (e.g., organizational behavior, college completion) could stop worrying about abstract theories such as Marxism or structural functionalism and instead focus on the puzzle solving required for particular topics. Another reason for middle-range theory's popularity is that sociology in the mid–twentieth century was quickly turning into a rich empirical field. Large-sample surveys were being fielded as early as the 1930s. Desktop computers later made it possible to analyze the massive amounts of data compiled through these surveys. By the late twentieth century, many sociologists didn't feel the need for another "grand" theory, but they did appreciate the need to develop lots of concrete hypotheses that could be tested with all these new data.

It might appear that the version of social theory I offer here is identical to Merton's middle-range theory because we both agree on the importance of empirical topics. But there are very important differences. First, I place a much stronger emphasis on "systematic" theory as a starting point for sociology. Middle-range theory, as Merton described it, can appear ad hoc and has the potential to flitter from topic to topic. The "network" of results may not have any obvious structure. In contrast, the approach I advocate, which focuses on the link between theories and mechanisms, starts with the view that topics and working hypotheses should be extracted from deeper insights. Sociology will be less ad hoc if the typical working hypothesis has some relation to a more expansive theory. Theory is what we get when we try to add order to the tangle of theories and hypotheses generated by topically oriented research. Second, building sociology from theories and their implied mechanisms more naturally fits the rhythm of science, which has cycles of theory building and hypothesis testing. Many "middle-range" sociologists are actively engaged with broader theory as they pursue their empirical research agendas.

If I am not promoting a version of Mertonian middle-range sociology, then what do I advocate? I think sociology is best described as a pluralistic field, an area of inquiry where it is normal to have competing and overlapping schools of thought. Each school of thought or style of social explanation is grounded in intuitions about social life and is capable of generating explanations in a wide range of environments. Thus, I believe that middle-range theory as a "network" of hypotheses doesn't quite capture much sociology as it is practiced today.[13] There definitely is a school of institutionalism that purports to offer a comprehensive explanation of how societies are organized. There definitely is an emerging comprehensive theory of inequality based on the work of Pierre Bourdieu and others. The purpose of this book is to break out of middle-range theory and show the reader the bigger conversation—the intuitions and broad insights that guide the modern sociologist.

The study of social capital illustrates the difference between mechanism-driven theory and middle-range sociology. The term *social capital* refers to the features of relationships that help people accomplish their financial or social goals such as finding a job. A woman who asks her friend for a business loan is relying on social capital. Because of their lifelong friendship, she is hoping her friend knows that she is a trustworthy. The middle-range sociologist might choose one case of social capital and study it, such as business ties among immigrants, whereas another sociologist might ask how people use social ties to find jobs out of high school. The middle-range sociologist would then try to generate a series of studies to help him or her determine if there are patterns to how people use social ties to achieve economic goals. The mechanism-based approach in this book takes a different track. First, the mechanism-based sociologist would ask how broad insights about social behavior can generate the links of cause and effect that characterize mechanisms. Second, he or she would survey the different mechanisms documented in research and then ask about commonalities and relate them to the basic ideas of sociology. Thus, a middle-range sociologist would be content to develop a theory of social capital, but the mechanism-based sociologist wants a conversation between social capital research, the explanations of behavior found in that research, and the "big" ideas of sociology. Indeed, this is exactly what happened in social capital research—there was a very long discussion in the field about whether social capital research supported or rejected strategic-action theory.[14]

This is but one example. Many other areas in sociology have a natural cycle of "middle-range research" that motivates or accompanies intensive investigation of a single topic while evaluating larger social theories. This is not unlike the approach to qualitative research that Iddo Tavory and Stefan Timmermans offer in their book *Abductive Analysis: Theorizing Qualitative Research* (2014). Also drawing on a pragmatist approach to social inquiry, Tavory and Timmermans suggest a cycle of investigating cases, revising prior beliefs, and integrating findings into the ideas of a larger research community.

FOUR APPROACHES TO SOCIOLOGY

In this section, I provide a more detailed description of the four major approaches to sociology that form the core of the book. The chapters that follow explore each approach in detail by examining its underlying assumptions and how it is used in highly influential sociological studies. Each chapter has a similar structure. I begin with a short example or observation that encapsulates an important sociological idea. Then I map the theoretical terrain. I describe the basic elements of the theory that formalizes the insight. Then I select specific examples of studies and theoretical arguments that illustrate the idea or provide background about its history and highlight interesting points.

Chapter 2 focuses on inequality and power. The intuition is fairly simple. In most societies, there appear to be groups of people who have more status than others. In medieval Europe, it was the nobility. In ancient China, it was the literati, an educated class of scholar-bureaucrats who came to have great power in the state. In modern society, we have people who command large incomes due to their position in industry. These groups acquire a disproportionate amount of resources and honor, and they actively attempt to perpetuate themselves.

The intuition behind "power and inequality" sociology is that some people have more status and influence than others. I have already mentioned one type of social theory, Marxism, that is built on the idea that society is best viewed as a struggle between people who manage to have control or ownership over industry and those who do manual work. But Marxism isn't the only theory of power and inequality that sociologists use. Other theories focus on gender or race as sources of social power and status. Much in the same way that a Marxist would try to explain school outcomes in terms of the privilege of wealthy children, a feminist sociologist might argue that men enjoy status privileges. What ties these ideas together is that they rely on the idea that one group enjoys extra benefits because of its ability to obtain extra money or status. Members of the group then use these resources to defend their position in society and to ensure that people in the group enjoy these same benefits.

In chapter 3, I discuss theories of strategic action, which try to explain how resources, knowledge, and social relationships affect our ability to achieve our goals. In this type of sociology, we often depict how people are faced with choices and must assess the costs and benefits of their actions. What college should

I go to? Whom should I marry? Whom should I hire for this job? Thus, one task for sociology is to understand the available choices and how people make decisions. Sociologists who work in this vein often employ the tools of an allied field, economics, to describe the choices that people make. Modern economics posits that behavior is driven by utility, the subjective value that people attach to the outcomes of their actions. This value may be monetary or symbolic, but as long as it leads to consistent rankings of options, it can explain behavior. Sociologists will sometimes adopt this approach in explaining people's choices. The choice of a spouse can be understood as utilizing cost–benefit analysis.

Resources are the other side of decisions and strategies. A consideration of resources is how sociologists in this field produce mechanisms. You can translate preferences into action only if you have specific tools, such as money or connections to employers. Any account of social behavior that doesn't explain where resources come from and how they are used is unsatisfactory. For example, protest movements don't have influence unless they have funds and organizations to back them up, a view called the "resource mobilization theory" of protest,[15] and the merchant may depend on the resources provided by friends, family, and partners. The sociologist's view of resources can be quite expansive, and a great deal of research in sociology tries to determine how social resources, such as personal connections, matter. Resources can be financial, social, or even symbolic. Regardless, much of sociology is motivated by the need to explain how these resources are created and used to achieve some tangible goal.

The next two approaches address more subtle but no less important issues. "Values and social structures" sociology, discussed in chapter 4, is an approach to sociology that focuses on the relationship between what people think is moral and legitimate, on the one hand, and the specific institutions and social practices that define a society, on the other. The fundamental intuition is that any specific organization or law or custom can't be sustained if everyone believes that it is not appropriate. Social structures must be consistent with social values. "Values and structures" sociology tends to use specific organizations, laws, practices, and policies to test and explore this idea. Some sociologists believe that there is a tight connection between social values and the institutions that people maintain. A school, for example, has to teach materials that the public deems legitimate. Alternative views suggest that organizations are only loosely connected to what the public wants. Organizations intentionally signal conformity to social norms but secretly carry on as they like. The enduring argument about the alleged power of norms over behavior is a defining feature of values and structure sociology.

The chapter on values and social structures also examines an area of inquiry now known as cultural sociology, which is an important subdiscipline of modern sociology. The hallmark of cultural sociology is its attempt to explain the ways that our collective ideas motivate and thus explain our actions. Cultural sociologists look at the structure of personal beliefs, how these beliefs are used by people to justify their actions, and how larger social forces shape individual beliefs. The reason that cultural sociology is included in a chapter about values and social structures is that it was originally developed as an alternative to earlier theories of social values. Cultural sociologists are less likely to understand people as assimilating social norms and more likely to view people as actively creating and using social rules. They see social behavior as more likely a reflection of social identities than as a rigid response to or rejection of norms.

The fourth major approach that I address in this book is social constructionism, which relies on a simple observation—group life is defined by conventions and collective belief. The law is powerful, but it is not much different than the rules one finds printed on the box of a board game. Both are arbitrary conventions designed to help people achieve some goal, whether it be resolving a dispute in civil court or helping children enjoy themselves. Both the law and board-game rules are created by people and not imposed by some higher power. Social constructionists try to understand everyday life as defined by perceptions, meanings, rules, and collective beliefs. It is an interaction guided by a frame, a set of meanings that indicates what is appropriate in a situation. People have rules that proscribe behavior in a particular circumstance. Social roles embody what people expect from others who occupy a specific position, such as boss or parent. Chapter 5 discusses frames, self-fulfilling prophecy, performativity, and the social creation of knowledge as examples of how broad ideas about social construction are applied in the study of specific social processes.

ILLUSTRATING THE "FOUR SOCIOLOGIES"

To help the reader understand the application of these ideas, each chapter is filled with examples of empirical analysis authored by sociologists and scholars in related fields. I have tried to stay away from a single topical area so that the reader doesn't think that the book is an exploration of a specialty within sociology, such as educational research or the sociology of the family. I also have made a conscious choice to include both newer and older examples of research. Certainly, one of this book's goals is to be contemporary in orientation, but age should not disqualify research from the discussion if it is a particularly good example for illustrating an idea. The book is not a compendium of recent breakthroughs. Rather, it is an attempt to present a set of core sociological ideas.

Inspired by this goal, I have selected examples based on the following criteria. First, some examples are included because they have become cornerstones of sociological analysis and are relevant to the four major themes discussed in this book. Ann Swidler's "tool kit" theory of social action, for example, is considered the beginning of modern studies of culture, so it fits very well into a discussion of values and social structure. In presenting her tool kit theory, Swidler responded directly to earlier sociologists' explanation of human action. Thus, a discussion of Swidler's argument is helpful for understanding a common argument in modern sociology as well as understanding how modern sociology has evolved from earlier sociology. Second, an empirical study might be discussed because it is a very distinctive example of a particular style of thought. In the chapter on strategic action, I discuss an article by Richard Breen and John H. Goldthorpe (1997) that uses decision theory to explain why young people from upper-class families are more likely to finish college. Although Breen and Goldthorpe's thesis is highly contested among educational researchers, it is a simple and clear example of how one can link social class to education outcomes using a rational-choice framework. Third, I want to break readers of the habit of reading sociology exclusively for the subjects of its inquiry and get them to think more about how sociologists generate explanations. If a chapter has examples from studies of stock markets and the campus hook-up culture, the reader should be able to assess how these seemingly disparate topics speak to common concerns. Variety can spur the intellect in valuable directions.

To further this goal, an appreciation of these four major currents of sociology and their corresponding theoretical recipes, each chapter has an orienting framework that helps the reader understand the interplay of big ideas and empirical examples, which can be relatively direct or complex. Chapter 2 addresses power and inequality, and the theme is the shift from older accounts of power focusing on overt intergroup conflict to more contemporary discussions that explore multiple forms of status and inequality and the often unconscious actions that perpetuate inequality. Chapter 3 is about strategic action. The narrative is straightforward. I begin with the simplest ideas about how people strategically act and then complicate the discussion by talking about how social context shapes the transition from individual preferences to social outcomes. Each example, then, is meant to show how simpler models of choice yield to sociologically richer models. Chapter 4 addresses an extremely broad tradition that asks how culture, individual action, and social structure are related. The examples are chosen to illustrate how some sociologists see a very tight link between values and structure, whereas other see a loose connection. Chapter 5 delves into social constructionism, and I pull together two major ideas from that tradition. Society emerges when people routinely gather and decide what is "real" for them. Thus, the examples in that chapter are chosen to address one of these sides of social construction or to pursue interesting aspects of the theory. Chapter 6 discusses how these different approaches or theories can be and are combined in contemporary sociology.

2

POWER AND INEQUALITY

I F Martians came to Earth to observe human societies, they might marvel at the differences between people. Some differences are physical: people vary in their complexion, their height, their gender, and their eye color. But these alien visitors might also find it interesting that people are socially unequal. Human beings vary a great deal in how much money they have and how much respect they command from each other. Our hypothetical visitors would find that some people are actively harassed. They suffer violence at the hands of others. They are mocked and humiliated. They are excluded from the best schools, the best jobs, and the nicest neighborhoods. In extreme cases, they are murdered and killed in brutal and dehumanizing ways.

Consider the case of African Americans in the era of Jim Crow, a time when American law and custom allowed whites to segregate blacks into separate schools, jobs, neighborhoods, and both public and private facilities. Simply being the descendant of a slave guaranteed that one would suffer a lifetime of harassment and humiliation. In nearly every way, blacks were abused and treated as second-class citizens. They did not have the right to vote, the right to marry whom they pleased, or even the right to travel from town to town without threat of violence.[1]

Education is an informative place to study the divergent lives of white and black Americans in detail. One of the main goals of American social policy after the Civil War was to create a system of separate schools for black and white students. Because U.S. federal law required that people be treated equally, the courts allowed states to provide "separate but equal" facilities. Of course, in practice, separate facilities were almost never equal in quality. The doctrine allowed states to claim equal treatment but permitted the facilities for black Americans to be much worse in practice.

Historian Louis Harlan provides an instructive overview of the situation in his book *Separate and Unequal: Public School and Racism in the Southern Seaboard States 1901–1915* (1968). In a discussion of North Carolina, considered by historians to be the *least* repressive of southern states, Harlan describes the massive imbalance between schools for whites and schools for blacks. Much of that imbalance started with funding. Roughly speaking, during the Jim Crow era, white schools received four dollars for every one dollar awarded to black schools.[2] Not surprisingly, white schools had a much lower student–teacher ratio. In poor areas, low funding levels meant a single school for white students and no school for blacks rather than a larger integrated school for both. And these were the *official* policies. Harlan reports that wealthy white school districts would often lobby the state government to covertly shift funds from black schools to white schools.

It should be no surprise that the physical facilities of black schools were horrible. Historians have described in detail the school buildings that were meant for black students.[3] Leaky roofs, poor construction, and insufficient supplies were the norm. Combined with the low student–teacher ratio, these schools were often holding pens for young people rather than places for learning. It shouldn't be a surprise that black intellectuals often viewed schools as a tool of social control instead of as an institution for progress.[4]

The segregated school system was only one aspect of a system of domination faced by blacks. In addition to state-sponsored segregation, there were informal forms of oppression, ranging from customs that required blacks to show deference to whites in public spaces to neighborhood segregation to brutal violence, including lynchings. The latter form of repression is notable not only for its inhumanity but also for its symbolic importance. These murders were meant to be seen as warnings to others who dared to violate the racial order of post–Civil War America.[5]

In the way that I describe it, the oppression of American blacks after the Civil War rested on two social processes. First, violence was used to harass blacks and exclude them from important resources, such as schools. In the case of schools, the violence refers to the coercive power of the state and how it was used to exclude blacks from educational institutions. In other cases, violence was expressed through the lynch mob. Second, there was a perpetual effort to denigrate blacks so that they would be associated with undesirable traits. For example, the custom of showing deference was intended to associate African Americans with being subservient. Scholars have repeatedly shown that in the media, even during Reconstruction, blacks were portrayed as criminal, deviant, and lazy.[6]

If we are to take the repression of blacks as an exemplar, then we would think that social inequality often results when one group uses violence, custom, and state policy to exclude another group from important opportunities and resources. In addition to normal variations in ability, personality, and temperament, inequality is also shaped by the relationship between larger groups in society, especially how superior groups relate to lower-status groups via violence and monopolization of resources. Superior status, in more traditional studies of inequality, emerges from overt intergroup conflict. In addition, we would be inclined to think that the dominant group would try to publicly tarnish the reputation of the inferior group and impose a stigma on them. Indeed, this is a valuable way to understand inequality and repression in many societies. Caste systems, such as India's, use law and custom to sort people into specific occupations. Low-status groups, such as untouchables, are required to perform undesirable tasks. These groups are subject to physical abuse, often with the wider society's tacit permission. For their entire lives, low-caste people must deal with the stigma associated with their social position and its permitted occupations.[7]

We might call this dual approach to inequality the "classical approach" because it appears so often in sociological work that seeks to understand repression. Marx, for example, famously argued that the bourgeoisie used the state to repress the revolutionary tendencies of the working classes, an analysis expanded on by later Marxists such as Louis Althusser. The analysis of white–black relations in this chapter is a thumbnail sketch of the theory offered by W. E. B. Du Bois in his analysis of the American South, *Black Reconstruction in America* ([1935] 1992). Scholars who focus on gender often begin by noting that women were often subject to law and custom that excluded them from schools and the professions and restricted property ownership. It is also the case that in many countries the law did not effectively punish men who harmed women.[8]

The purpose of this chapter is to explain how theories of inequality have moved beyond this classical approach by examining key works in the study of race, gender, and social class. Recent scholars have shifted away from classical explanations that rely on intergroup conflict, competition, and repression and have adopted a new explanatory approach that focuses on privilege and superior exploitation of social resources. Starting in the 1970s, most notably with the work of Pierre Bourdieu, sociologists working in a range of areas formulated a new, contemporary approach to inequality that relies on ideas such as habitus, symbolic capital, and unconscious racism. The issue is that the sorts of social processes described by Marx, Weber, Du Bois, feminist writers such as Simone de Beauvoir, and others are no longer seen as adequate models of how inequality emerges and is perpetuated in modern society.

Take schooling, for example. It is no longer the case that blacks are literally barred from white schools as in the Jim Crow era. Instead, American schools seem eager to present themselves as "multicultural," which means that they celebrate and promote ethnic diversity. Similarly, women used to be segregated from men in schools and colleges. Many professional schools refused, on principle, to admit more than a few women per year to study law or medicine. Now, the situation is reversed. There are many professions where women are the majority. For example, the legal profession is now approaching a point where women outnumber men in law schools. In recent years, the number of female medical school graduates has now reached parity with the number of male graduates.[9]

Despite these welcome changes in American society, there remains a great deal of inequality. African Americans still have worse life-course outcomes. They are less likely to go to college, enter the professions, and accumulate wealth. African Americans suffer more stress, have more cardiac disease, and have more problems accessing medical care.[10] They are, moreover, subject to mass incarceration in the United States. There is also enduring inequality with respect to gender so that gaps in education, income, and careers between men and women still remain.

And although our society has produced enormous wealth, people with low incomes still have very different life outcomes than do people who are born to families of great wealth.

In the face of such facts, the classical theory of inequality needs serious modification. A new theory needs to focus less on overt forms of physical and symbolic violence while acknowledging that they are still important. It needs to admit that the average African American in 2016 faces substantially different conditions than her ancestor in 1916. Such a revised theory would have to explain how it is that overt forms of repression, such as lynching or the exclusion of women from the professions, have to a considerable extent been replaced by new social processes that underwrite racial differences. The successor theory would need to offer a new mechanism for explaining enduring inequality. It would have to explain why a society that claims to be color blind and gender neutral creates a world where race and gender matter so much in predicting the course of one's life.

THE NEW THEORY OF INEQUALITY

This chapter outlines a new theory of inequality that has arisen from analyzing the social and racial hierarchies that characterize modern American life. In my view, these analyses are responses to empirical observations and proposed mechanisms that link group identity to unequal life outcomes. First, there has been a widespread shift from conscious and blatant forms of discrimination to more subtle, unconscious forms of discrimination. It is much less common than it once was for people to explicitly articulate highly visible attacks on other groups. People are instead often motivated by moods or gut feelings about the merit or moral worth of people from other groups. In the American context, it is much less likely that people consciously subscribe to the idea that low-status ethnic groups, such as migrants, are lazy or criminal or that they will justify their actions on an explicit ideology of racial inferiority. Rather, Americans tend to rely on a deep-seated but often unconscious ideology that depicts low-status groups as responsible for their own problems and downplays any role that high-status groups have in perpetuating inequality. This is a very different account of inequality than, say, the one that Du Bois presented in his analysis of the American South, which drew attention to violence and the psychological benefits that whites received from seeing themselves as superior to blacks. Modern theories posit a new psychology of racial difference.

Second, groups can now maintain their relative advantage without resorting to explicit violence or social regulation. Earlier scholars spent a great deal of time explaining all the different ways that American whites harassed blacks or mobilized the state to defend their privilege. Numerous books describe slavery, violence (e.g., lynchings), segregation in schools, exclusion from state and federal jobs, and so forth. But now these forms of oppression are abolished, banned by law, mitigated, or relatively rare. This is not to say that violence never occurs. Rather, the primary mechanism for inequality is to be found elsewhere. Specifically, a number of researchers argue that groups maintain their advantage by virtue of their knowledge of institutions such as school or government, their comfort with mainstream cultures, and their "inside connections." In other words, if one wants to know why on average black students don't do as well as their white counterparts, one is not likely to be offered an explanation based on Jim Crow–style segregation. One will instead hear explanations that discuss issues such as the differences between white and black networks, the conflicts between white teachers and black students, and the fact that white students appear to know about the "unwritten" rules of the school.

The new theory of inequality is built around a few ideas that allow researchers to develop explanations of racism or sexism in this new social environment. One of the main ideas is that human beings have distinctive bundles of attitudes and moods that motivate and orient their behavior with other people. These bundles of attitudes, which the French sociologist Pierre Bourdieu called "habitus," emerge from specific institutional contexts and reflect the values embodied by these institutions. The teacher, for example, focuses on caring for people and has automatic "gut" responses to students, parents, and administrators. Similarly, the habitus can have racialized or gendered components. People have intuitions or ways of prejudging others that reflect social hierarchies. It is "obvious" that some people are deserving of economic assistance and equal job opportunities, but others are not. It is also argued that people vary in their ability to exploit their institutional context and that this variation is tied to habitus as well. Therefore, inequality need not be tied to direct intergroup conflict. The first-generation college student, for example, may feel uncomfortable on a university campus and alienated from its teachers and administrators. In contrast, the child of middle-class professionals can more easily talk with and bargain with professors, administrators, and others who give out rewards on college campuses. By relying on unconscious attitudes and unequal levels of social skill, the new theory of inequality is able to address how inequality persists in a nation where discrimination against minorities and women is castigated and, in many cases, illegal.

The new theory of inequality isn't without alternatives. A book that seeks to outline social theory broadly as it is expressed in empirical research can't cover all rival theories, but I can discuss a few of them. I call one alternative to the new theory of inequality the "violence by other means" theory of domination. A number of scholars have argued that violence remains one of the very important mechanisms for inequality, but it is disguised by the legal system. It isn't about mobs lynching those they want to control or the police just arbitrarily sweeping up crowds of people at a labor rally. Rather, it's about creating a system of state repression that appears to be unrelated to an individual's status but in practice has its most onerous effects on low-status populations. This alternate approach to inequality, the "violence by other means" theory, has many roots. In American sociology, it has often been inspired by the mass incarceration begun in the 1980s and continuing to this day. For this theory, many scholars draw upon the writings of Michel Foucault and others, who have claimed that Western societies have gradually built up a vast system for controlling, punishing, and jailing many of its citizens.

A second alternative is intersectionality theory, which builds on prior research in race, gender, and social class. With antecedents in classical social theory, intersectionality theory bridges older inequality theory with a modern approach. Relying on the observation that inequality is defined in multiple ways, intersectionality theory draws attention to the social spaces created by the simultaneous application of multiple categories. In terms of the overall movement of inequality theory in sociology, I situate this theory as one that reformulates, rearticulates, and extends the ideas of classical sociology.

The rest of this chapter begins with a summary of intersectionality research, which can be seen as a theory that merges contemporary approaches to race and gender with older views of status. Then I present Bourdieu's theory of power and inequality because his work uniquely synthesizes these arguments about the social psychology of privilege, the struggle for status and position, and the manipulation of resources. This chapter shows how these ideas have motivated further research on inequality. I discuss three exemplars: Annette Lareau's explanation of why working-class

children don't excel in school; Eduardo Bonilla-Silva's exploration of "color-blind racism"; and Cecilia Ridgeway's recent theory
of gendered stereotypes. Finally, I devote some space to the "violence by other means" theory. That section begins with a review
of Foucault's theory of the punitive society and concludes with a
brief discussion of the theory regarding mass incarceration.

CLASSICAL INEQUALITY THEORY AND THE
JUMP TO INTERSECTIONALITY

This chapter began with a gruesome review of the conditions
faced by African Americans in the age of racial segregation. Not
surprisingly, the writers who defined the basic language of sociology in the late nineteenth and early twentieth centuries viewed
power and status in terms of physical and symbolic violence.
Students often read Du Bois's unforgettable description of the
post-Reconstruction South and its many rules of racial deference,
which were enforced by legal sanctions, threats, intimidation, and
lynchings.[11] If a black man in the South did not offer the "proper"
level of respect to a white man or woman he encountered, he
would be mocked, humiliated, or even murdered. Similarly, many
sociologists of gender have described how men in many societies engage in violence against women. Many students of gender,
such as anthropologist Gayle Rubin, have further argued that
women in many societies are essentially treated as property to be
exchanged for status and favors.[12] What these arguments have in
common is that a single well-defined category, such as "female" or
"working class," motivates the analysis.

During the twentieth century, theorists' tendency to focus
on one category of inequality (e.g., "female" or "white") began
to weaken. For example, by the 1950s E. Franklin Frazier wrote

eloquently about the "black bourgeoisie."[13] The essence of Frazier's argument was that African Americans of high social class were caught in a no man's land—above the average African American yet unable to fully participate in white culture. The pivotal theoretical move that Frazier makes and that was absent in the work of earlier writers such as Du Bois, Weber, and Marx is that the combination of social class and race creates a unique position in the American social structure. Members of a low-status group who accumulate wealth rise above their peers, but this resource is not enough to overcome the cultural barriers that whites set up.

In the 1960s, intersectionality began to emerge as a major idea among scholars. A dispute among feminist theorists precipitated this theory. Specifically, a number of black feminists argued that feminism as a political and social movement was overly dominated by the views of middle-class white women.[14] Although originally a statement about the relationship of political feminism to its constituency, this critique offered an implicit social theory. There are multiple forms of inequality, and their interactions create a highly complex social structure with communities that have unique experiences. Thus, in the context of second-wave feminism, it was crucial to assert that women have highly diverse experiences and that feminism should seriously address all types of women's experiences, not just those of more privileged white women.

This observation was brought into modern academic sociology most notably through the writings of Patricia Hill Collins. Starting with the observation that black women have a different social position, a position of relative marginality, Collins argued that there is a "matrix of domination."[15] In American society, people are categorized by a three-dimensional status system that combines race, gender, and class. A number of powerful conclusions follow from this basic idea. One is positional. There is not just a dichotomy between men and women or between blacks and whites. Rather, many "boxes" combine multiple traits and reflect distinct historical experiences. A second conclusion is that life-course outcomes will vary not only by race or class but also by combinations of these traits.

Here, I would like to elaborate on why intersectionality theory is an important advance over classical theories of power and inequality. Perhaps the most important point is that intersectionality theory has a more systematic and complex description of status in society. In older theory, one would take a single dimension of inequality and study it in relative isolation. A classical scholar of race, for example, might talk about the meaning of race or the effects of racial differences on college graduation or income. In contrast, intersectionality theorists start with the assumption that societies have multiple, interrelated dimensions of inequality and the different aspects of status combine in possibly unique ways. Thus, intersectionality theory is an intuitive way to understand that social inequality is not uniform and doesn't always operate in the same way for all people. One must translate the macrosociological status orders into specific situations and be attuned to the complexities they entail. To study race and college graduation in America, one must not only account for race but also recognize that not all African Americans have the same college experience. The time spent in college and the ability to finish a college degree are also influenced by a student's personal wealth, gender, and other forms of status. To rework Frazier's example, a low-income African American person and a high-income African American person will have different outcomes because of his or her different relationships to the mainstream culture.

A related point is that intersectional theory offers an interesting approach to social position. In older theory, it is often assumed that women or ethnic minorities or working-class people are always at a disadvantage in all situations. In contrast, intersectionality theory suggests that there are different situations, and salient forms of status will change according to the context. Patricia Hill Collins noted this in her discussion of race, class, and gender. African American men might experience disadvantage at work because of their ethnicity but a superior position at home because of their gender. Once again, college education provides an interesting example. A wealthy African American student might experience conflict with white students in the dormitory but still have access to good jobs due to his or her family's wealth. Collins made the additional point that some positions are so distinct that they encourage a unique form of consciousness. Drawing on this insight, she argued that minority women, especially African American women, have a unique perspective on society due to their low position along all dimensions of status.

Since the publication of Collins's seminal writings on the topic, an entire generation of sociologists has expanded and elaborated on her ideas. For example, recent ethnographic studies of health and inequality have used intersectionality theory to understand the subtleties of access to health care. In a study of how people access reproductive-health services in Harlem, Leith Mullings and Alaka Wali examine how gender and class come together to constrain people as they seek those services.[16] Following about two dozen women over a two-year period, Mullings and Wali explore how class shapes and constrains their actions. The findings are nuanced, but they consistently indicate how class shapes African American women's ability to find emotional, social, and economic support. The type of job that these women have, a marker of social class, often affects how much stress they experience because some jobs help women obtain access to resources that allow them to solve problems concerning child birth and reproductive health, but some jobs do not. Drawing on intersectionality's main insight, Mullings and Wali conjecture that African American women develop a distinct coping strategy that might be deleterious. Responding to the dual forces of racial and economic inequality, "Sojourner Syndrome" occurs when African American women actively cope with stressors and this active coping "interacts with low socioeconomic status to influence the[ir] health." The syndrome name refers to nineteenth-century activist Sojourner Truth, who in a famous speech asserted her strength and equality with men in the face of constant discrimination and repression. Mullings and Wali further explain: "The Sojourner Syndrome expresses the combined effects and joint influence of race, class, and gender in structuring risk for African American women. . . . This framework may help to clarify the mechanism by which race mediates both gender and status. First, the consequences of race and gender—of being a black woman—contribute to the instability of class status. . . . [M]iddle stratum black women have attained the achievements necessary for middle class status, but they continue to suffer job and occupational discrimination."[17] A very specific social position subjects African American women to additional stress, which results in a potentially debilitating pattern of overcompensation.

Intersectionality is useful not only for describing inequality but also for thinking about social change. Political groups often rely on the resources that come from the combination of ethnic, economic, and sexual identities. In a recent study of youth activism, Veronica Terriquez argues that movements can exhibit "intersectional mobilization."[18] There are times when a mobilized constituency has inequality within it, and a marginalized group within a larger movement can use its hardship to amplify its voice. Terriquez uses the example of lesbian, gay, bisexual, and transgender (LGBT) participants in youth movements. Queer young people can use their personal experiences of hardship to deepen the broader commitment to their cause. Terriquez notes that immigrant youth groups often have LGBT leaders who are emboldened by the proposed DREAM Act (Development, Relief, and Education for Alien Minors), which would offer legal protections to undocumented youth who were brought to the United States as minors. Thus, the combination of migration status and sexuality facilitates the emergence of a queer leadership among immigrant youth groups. Jennifer Jihye Chun, George Lipsitz, and Young Shin draw attention to a related process— how intersectionality might be conducive to social change.[19] In their study of Asian Immigrant Women Advocates, a Bay Area migrant-rights group, they show that the organization could empower women to become more educated by appealing both to nationality and to social class. Their study of this group focuses on how its campaigns relied on simultaneous appeals to Asian pan ethnicity and workers' rights. These campaigns helped migrant women become more educated and extract more concessions in the work place, such as addressing dangerous job conditions in the Bay Area garment industry.

Here, the goal is to discuss how intersectionality builds on prior sociological ideas about race, class, and gender. Collins's prime insight and empirical work by scholars such as Mullings, Wali, Terriquez, Chun, Lipsitz, and Shin build on a century of work on the nature of race and gender as a social category. In my view, intersectionality theory presents a path of intellectual development that neither hews to older views, such as orthodox Marxism, nor formulates completely new mechanisms. Rather, it is a subtle yet powerful reworking of long-standing ideas about status that pays close attention to the tensions present in any system of inequality. An individual often has a position of dominance according to one dimension of inequality but not according to other dimensions. Those with a low status in many dimensions are in a unique position to critique the matrix of domination, whereas those with a higher position enjoy reinforcing the privilege they possess. The next section discusses a quite different approach to inequality that still refers to traditional ideas of race and class but embeds these ideas in a newer structural argument about how societies are put together.

HIERARCHIES, FIELDS, AND RESOURCES

Intersectionality theory is an extension of classical theories of inequality that focused on specific forms of status, such as race, gender, and social class. The new theory of inequality offers a different approach to studying power and status in a society. Roughly speaking, society is seen as a cluster of interconnected fields, such as education or government, and each field has its own resources and mindset. Thus, to understand inequality, one should try to understand how each field is organized, how people can achieve status or position in that field, and why some groups systematically come out on top. The social theorist who is most well known for promoting this approach to inequality is Pierre Bourdieu, a scholar who has had a deep influence on the social sciences. Originally trained in philosophy, Bourdieu began producing ethnographic accounts of tribal life in Algeria and later wrote seminal analyses of French social and political life. Covering a wide range of topics, from the French university system to the fine arts, Bourdieu's analyses share a common interest in the interrelated topics of power, social organization, and status.

In presenting the underlying ideas of Bourdieu's approach, it helps to begin with a discussion of his theory of the social field as presented in *An Outline of Theory of Practice* (1977) and other works.[20] Bourdieu claims that a social domain (field), such as school or the art world, is a realm with its own resources and hierarchies. In education, prestige and honor go to those who master certain kinds of knowledge and possess specific kinds of resources, such as degrees or university affiliations. The degree confers a level of honor to a person and is often associated with higher lifetime earnings. College degrees are also seen as prerequisites for further training, especially in the professions, and it is very difficult to command political authority in modern societies without higher education. Within the university system, there are forms of status, as indicated by ubiquitous college rankings. Gaining admission to a highly regarded school can bolster one's position in the world of education. In other words, every social "world" comes equipped with a ranking system that "everybody" knows about and with specific things (symbolic capital) that are considered resources within that system.

What makes Bourdieu's theory distinctive is that he provides readers with an interesting social psychology. Associated with each field is a "habitus," a set of preferences, moods, and dispositions. The word *disposition* is central to the theory. It isn't always the case that people have an explicit ideology or theoretical system that justifies their beliefs. Rather, these beliefs work "from the gut." The people who inhabit Bourdieu's theory resemble in many ways our commonsense view of how people reason in everyday situations. People have emotion-laced intuitions about how the world operates and what is proper. What Bourdieu adds is that these intuitions reflect the structure of fields and enable their reproduction. People's tacit understanding of the world is an understanding of inequality, how it is justified, and how to gain position in that world.

Take voting, for example. One might assume, as do many political scientists, that voting represents an obvious translation of interests into votes. The person who wants more taxes is more likely to vote for a candidate who says that he or she will raise taxes. However, studies of voters show that people in general know very little about specific candidates and that they often hold inconsistent policy preferences (e.g., some voters want to expand government while lowering taxes).[21] Yet even though voters don't appear to be knowledgeable about candidates or even have consistent policy ideas, they tend to have very firm preferences. Some voters, for example, will vote for a single party, no matter what, even if the party drops a once popular policy position, such as a Democratic candidate who promises to lower taxes or a Republican who promises to cut defense spending.[22] What this suggests is that voting reflects a person's alliance with a party that represents an idea rather than carefully considered policy analysis. In American politics, for example, those who side with minorities might gravitate toward the Democratic Party, whereas those who think minorities have invalid grievances tend to align with the rival Republican Party. Thus, electoral politics may reflect cheerleading for a team, a habitus in the voting booth.

Bourdieu's theory succinctly brings together the issues that define the contemporary study of hierarchies and power in sociology. The trinity of field, habitus, and symbolic capital captures the inner logic of a particular domain. Social position within a community depends on how well one masters and internalizes the rules of the game. Playing the game also means perpetuating the inequalities associated with that social domain. As we play the game, we make the game seem normal, and we teach it to others. The idea of habitus encapsulates the psychology of status. The drive for status has concrete benefits, but it also provides an identity for a person. Thus, people have a deeply rooted interest in playing the game and enforcing its rules.

This theory expands previous inequality theory in two very important ways. First, it is highly general. Any social domain may be defined as a field. A casual perusal of contemporary sociology shows the flexibility of the idea. Bourdieu himself applied the idea to the worlds of government,[23] academia,[24] and the fine arts.[25] Others have applied the theory to primary schools,[26] the avant-garde jazz scene of the 1960s,[27] ethnic studies,[28] the mortgage industry,[29] and international law.[30] Thus, inequality theory is no longer confined to situations defined by commerce or politics. As long as human beings vie for status and establish identity according to rules, social actions may be described in Bourdieu's terms. The worlds of art, the law, academia, and the state can be viewed as fields as long as one recognizes how each field possesses its own distinct form of *capital*, Bourdieu's term for resources associated with that field.

Second, Bourdieu added a social psychology that was missing or underdeveloped in earlier theory. Earlier theorists had often relied on either a psychology of resistance or a psychology of co-optation. That is, when sociologists discussed the psychology of inequality, they tended to focus on how people came to see themselves as superior and how repressed people came to believe that this state of affairs is unjust. This, for example, is a typical approach in the study of social movements, which often touches on studies of "oppositional consciousness."[31] In these studies, the term *oppositional consciousness* denotes the ideas that people acquire as they develop a political grievance. There is much discussion of how people come to view the status quo as illegitimate and of the hothouse environment within movements.[32] Another psychological approach draws on Marx's classic claim that people are co-opted by the system that represses them. Subjugation entails a sort of self-enslavement, wherein oppressed people, be it the working class, women, or minorities, come to see their inferior position as completely natural, perhaps the just outcome of their undesirable behavior. Marx referred to this co-optation as "false consciousness." Anticolonialists, such as Franz Fanon, later called it the "settler mentality."[33]

Habitus and field theory takes a somewhat different approach. The idea of habitus focuses on the individual's relation to her entire field, the resources she possesses, and how skillfully she deploys them. Rather than view an individual as consciously repressing others, habitus theory depicts individuals who are completely socialized into some institutional system. There is no need to repress others if everyone accepts the rules of the game. In much the same way that a chess master does not "repress" lower-skilled chess players, people of a higher social class do not need to forcibly dominate others. They maintain their relative position because of superior resources and skills, and the "players" accept the rules of the game. The child of a wealthy family succeeds in school not because she undermines the performance of others. She succeeds because her family provides the knowledge and cultural skills needed to succeed in school. The child and parents have internalized the values of the school in ways that children from working-class families have not.

It is instructive to contrast this view with Du Bois's racial wage theory, which asserted that southern whites tolerated their poverty only because they derived satisfaction from nevertheless being seen as superior to blacks. The Du Boisian theory implies that whites have a well-developed theory of race. In the post-Reconstruction South, whites clearly believed that blacks were morally defective, and they openly endorsed treating people differently because of their race. Historians of that era have even documented the attempt to justify racist policies by appeals to crime statistics and other social trends.[34] In comparison, habitus theory suggests a very different psychology. As discussed in more detail later in this chapter, whites, in Bourdieu's theory, can still perpetuate inequality without claiming that blacks are inferior. In fact, Bourdieu's theory allows for the possibility that whites genuinely believe blacks are their equals and that whites would be made uncomfortable by the mere thought of racism. Bourdieu would focus instead on the moods and dispositions that motivate people to prefer people of the same ethnic group without needing an explicit ideology of racism.

The next two sections examine how this intellectual apparatus has been applied to contemporary studies of inequality. I first explore the idea of habitus and field in a discussion of Annette Lareau's book *Unequal Childhoods: Class, Race, and Family Life* (2003), a text that shows in detail how working-class and middle-class children have different cognitive and emotional orientations toward schools. Then I explore Eduardo Bonilla-Silva's work *Racism Without Racists* (2014), which has become a seminal treatment of how people's unarticulated beliefs about race can justify and promote racist behavior.

A Habitus Approach to Schooling

One of the most vivid applications of Bourdieu's theory in recent sociology is *Unequal Childhoods* (2003) by Annette Lareau. Drawing from two years of ethnographic observations of parents, children, and their schools, Lareau documents how parents assist their children in schools. Her point is not merely that some parents are more involved than others or that some parents have more money. Many researchers have already made these points. Rather, she argues that parents have a specific mindset that guides how they help their children. This mindset—or habitus, as Bourdieu puts it—varies by social class. Educated parents have internalized the logic of the school bureaucracy. When their children encounter problems, more-educated parents know how to game the school better than their less-educated counterparts do. They "just know" how to work with the teachers in order to give their children the best education. In contrast, less-educated working-class parents don't completely understand the working of the school and are much less likely to show savvy when dealing with teachers and administrators.

In a very interesting passage, Lareau describes what different kinds of parents know about their children's daily lives.[35] Reflecting a belief that children must have structured schedules that enrich them through endless activities, middle- and upper-class parents possess a detailed knowledge of what their children do nearly every hour of the day. The more-educated parents can easily recite entire daily schedules and summarize the homework that their children must do, and they know what the child is succeeding or failing at. In contrast, less-educated parents, who are often in working-class occupations, are not aware as much of their children's lives in as much detail. One parent reported she wasn't even certain of what classes her child was taking. This observation is not meant to disparage working-class parents. It is hard for parents who work long hours to spend the time needed to learn about their child's school and classes in such detail. More importantly, the distinction is the result of a different life course. Middle-class parents, who are likely college educated, have years of experience dealing with colleges, businesses, and all sort of institutions. Thus, "hovering" over their child is relatively easy. They rely on a lifetime of experience. Working-class parents, who may have little education beyond high school, don't have a body of knowledge that they can quickly tap into as they make sense of the often arcane world of American schools.

Lareau's discussion is remarkable not just because it shows how parents' education is a crucial resource for creating future inequality but also because it draws attention to the precise moments where the inequalities emerge. Traditionally, a student of inequality might argue that education is linked to class because more-educated parents might send their children to better schools.[36] Another such traditional argument is that schooling is designed, perhaps unintentionally, to favor students from more comfortable backgrounds, an argument promoted by British sociologist Basil Bernstein, who often pointed out that schools teach in ways that can alienate working-class children.[37] Paul Willis, in *Learning to Labor* (1981), went further to argue that the purpose of the school system was to train working-class students to be laborers and to maintain their class position.

Lareau's arguments are different. Even if a school were operated in a way to reduce class biases, children from educated families would still do better. They have an ingrained sense of how a bureaucratic system works that can help their children succeed. They know how to push arguments with teachers and know what the best tracks are within the school. This is a psychological argument about how people achieve their goals. Older theories of inequality assumed that individuals from different classes understand the world in the same way but that the lower class is prevented from the exploiting the opportunities given to them. The new theory of inequality, especially that produced by Bourdieu and his followers, provides a different story. Working-class people may perceive institutions in fundamentally different ways than upper-class people. For working-class people, life in school or at work or in other contexts is often about order and obedience to authority. For middle- and upper-class people, institutional life is a never-ending series of games and negotiations. The teacher's grades aren't a final judgment. For wealthier kids, grades are the opening round of a bargaining game that some children know how to play, but for others the game is one they shouldn't even bother to join.

Lareau's analysis can also help us understand the politics of schools, not just the distribution of outcomes. For example, there has been much contention over No Child Left Behind, a law passed in 2001 that requires schools to meet standardized testing goals. As discussed in more detail in chapter 4, teachers strongly resist this law. Here, I discuss one way of explaining this resistance using Lareau's ideas. Although it is undoubtedly true that standardized tests are a challenge to a teacher's autonomy, they might also disrupt the student's ability to bargain with their teachers. Similarly, they prevent adults from effectively coaching their children. Tests are graded by an impersonal computer. Appeals are rare and difficult to win. Standardized tests rob students, parents, and teachers of an opportunity to assert themselves and to gain control over how children are evaluated. The alternative, coaching students in test taking, is much more difficult and risky. In a society that values individuality, an impersonal system of evaluation must feel like a profound violation of the right to argue with the referee. Not surprisingly, recent school ethnographies have focused on how standardized tests create emotional turmoil among teachers because it disrupts the way that things have always been done.[38]

The differences between working-class kids and middle- and upper-class kids continue into college. Other scholars have documented the numerous ways that students from working-class backgrounds fail to take advantage of their college experience. These students often feel uncomfortable in an environment where other students visibly show their wealth, and they are less likely to participate in extracurricular activities, professional networking events, and so forth. Recent work by Elizabeth Armstrong and Laura Hamilton illustrates this point in great detail. In a multiyear ethnographic study of a midwestern research university, Armstrong and Hamilton followed a cohort of women enrolled in the school.[39] What they found is that social class strongly shaped these women's experiences. Well-to-do students have the time and money to pursue extracurricular activities. In general, upper-class students have more flexibility in their budgets and schedules, which allows them to get the most from their college experience. But there are also cognitive differences. Women from more privileged families tend to see college as another example of self-cultivation, which drives them to seek experiences that reinforce this image. Like their primary-school counterparts, working-class college students see college in much more functional terms. This behavior has consequences. Spending time working multiple jobs and not taking part in extracurricular activities decreases the chance that a student will make the sorts of connections with faculty and other students that might help him or her later in life.

These multiple studies of education sharply draw our attention to the "invisible curriculum" of the school and college. Modern stratification researchers now appreciate that the mastery of the unwritten rules matters and that success isn't merely a question of knowledge. Some people, due to their life experiences, have a stronger intuitive sense of how institutions work and what it takes to get ahead. The message of the new inequality theory is broad. It suggests that any institutional environment, such as a university, will provide advantages to those who understand its unwritten code. Schools have an unwritten curriculum; jobs have unwritten rules. Everything has unwritten rules! The differences we see in outcomes probably depend on how people intuitively grasp their social world, which, as Lareau, Armstrong, Hamilton, and others have shown, in turn depends a great deal on social class.

"Racism Without Racists"

Habitus is a subtle but powerful element of the new theory of inequality. It isn't quite an attitude, like approving of divorce, and it isn't always clearly expressed, like having a political ideology (e.g., environmentalism or libertarianism). Habitus is a "disposition." One might infer that habitus is the hidden engineer who guides the mind. It might be viewed as a socially shaped sense of self that provides both meaning (What's going on here?) and direction (What should I do?). One might argue that habitus theory is broader than either the tool kit theory of culture (see chapter 4) or the decision maker of rational-choice theory (see chapter 3). The habitus certainly includes strategies for dealing with the world, which Bourdieu calls practice, but the theory further suggests that people's disposition enables them to create a folk epistemology or a way of categorizing the world that makes sense, and this system allows them to gather the things that they need to strive for position.

In a book titled *Racism Without Racists: Color-Blind Racism and the Persistence of Racial Inequality in America* (2014), Eduardo Bonilla-Silva argues that the inequality between blacks and whites is maintained by a very specific habitus that presents itself as a color-blind ideology and thus makes it difficult for people to question the legitimacy of racial inequality. Bonilla-Silva's analysis focuses on four different cognitive strategies that whites and blacks to some degree use when discussing race: "abstract liberalism" (not using force to address racial inequality), "naturalization" (suggesting racial differences are normal), "minimization" (suggesting racism is of little practical importance), and "cultural racism" (ascribing negative outcomes to choices made by certain ethnic groups).[40] Taken together, these four framings allow individuals to avoid addressing discrimination and considering policies that might mitigate racial inequality.

It is worth comparing Bonilla-Silva's assumptions with those made by of earlier theorists. Bonilla-Silva does not start with the assumption that individuals have a clearly articulated racial ideology. As mentioned earlier, when Du Bois wrote about segregation in the South, he argued that working-class whites were willing to accept their poor conditions because they enjoyed deference from blacks. Du Bois noted that this sense of entitlement was not only expressed on an interpersonal level but also broadcast in the media, which portrayed blacks in a sensationalist manner. Similarly, Edward Said, the Palestinian American literary scholar, argued that Western society's engagement with the Islamic world is defined by a particular ideology that emphasizes the exoticness of non-Western cultures.[41]

Bonilla-Silva's argument takes a different approach. The creation and continuation of racial differences do not require an explicit consciousness on the behalf of any particular group. All one needs is an explanation of how it is that people can claim to be neutral toward race or even celebrate racial diversity but at the same time remain tolerant of significant levels of discrimination and unequal life outcomes. For example, Bonilla-Silva argues that claiming the "end of racism" allows members of the dominant group to continue enjoying their privileges because there will be no opportunity for others to challenge these privileges. That is, if two groups, such as American blacks and whites, have highly different experiences, it is to the benefit of the superior group simply to claim that prejudice no longer happens, which shifts responsibility to the subordinate group to prove that they are subject to discrimination.

The "racism without racists" theory is at its core about the social psychology of being white. It is about the dispositions and values held by members of the dominant racial group and their superior institutional resources. What Bonilla-Silva adds in this case is an argument about the totalizing nature of these differences and how they interact with other forms of capital in American society. Ideas about what is fair and whether racism persists allow certain groups to maintain an advantage in job opportunities, schooling, and public life. For Bonilla-Silva, racialization is such a fundamental phenomenon that it affects all other social domains. The minimization of minorities' achieve-ments occurs not only during schooling but also within the work-place and in cultural areas. Thus, race is a factor in the creation of all other resources. It is not possible to completely separate economic resources or educational credentials or other forms of capital from a society's system of racial categories.

GENDER

In modern sociology, gender is considered one of the major fac-tors in creating and sustaining inequality. Gender is empirically correlated with many important major life-course outcomes. For example, American women on average earn less income than men.[42] They are less likely to hold positions of authority, such as elected office, or top management positions in for-profit firms.[43] In some cases, however, women appear to do better than their male counterparts—for example, on measures of health and in terms of schooling. Women are more likely to finish high school and college, and their numbers now equal that of men in many professions.[44] Thus, sociologists of gender face an empirical puz-zle. They must account for the fact that women are on average paid less in the labor market even while they are making notice-able gains in schooling and other areas.

Like sociologists who study race and class, sociologists of gender have offered their own theory of a gendered habitus. It is common among sociologists to talk about "doing gender," which means to actively behave in ways that are considered ste-reotypically feminine or masculine.[45] One might use this sort of theoretical lens when reading studies that argue that women do not achieve as much as men in the professions because of social-ization. One common argument is that some occupations have become typed as masculine or feminine. This claim, for example, is often found in the literature on gender gaps in science. Observing that women are considerably underrepresented in the physical sciences and engineering, numerous scholars have argued that women are taught that science is unfeminine. A related argument is that women do not reach positions of high status in the physical sciences because few hold positions of leadership in those fields. The paucity of women in these fields makes the environment inhospitable to female entrants because there are fewer women to network with and fewer female role models.[46]

Another strand of research that might be viewed as an investigation of how gender plays out in various social fields is the research on labor markets that focuses on gendered segregation of jobs. The empirical observation is that many occupations tend to be segregated by gender. Many jobs tend to be performed by overwhelming numbers of women (e.g., nursing) or men (e.g., construction work). This is striking in the modern age because many jobs, such as nursing, can easily be done by individuals of any gender. Arguments about the gendered segregation of occupations are many, and the literature is complex, but one can start by noting that legal and administrative barriers are now gone, with some exceptions—for instance, in soldiering. What is interesting about this massive literature is that its different parts speak to different aspects of social fields. One part of the literature, for example, talks about a job's image—men don't go into nursing because it appears feminine to them.[47] Another part talks about the emotional content of work. Jobs that require caring for others attract women because they are taught, since youth, to be more outwardly caring, a view compatible with the idea that women are more responsible for family and child raising.[48]

One thing that modern research on gender shares with the arguments about race and class is a movement away from brute force and state sanction as a principal explanation for why gender inequalities persist. The mechanisms found in many modern studies of gender describe how men and women differently interact with the institutions of modern society, how people ascribe traits to men and women, and how men and women have different levels of access to different resources needed to succeed.

The new theory of inequality can't be applied to gender without modification. The inequality related to gender has features that are distinct and merits its own theoretical consideration. The first distinct feature is that the processes that shape gender-based inequality are often tied to the family in extremely important ways. For example, what happens at work is often affected by how men and women settle the household division of labor. The number of hours spent on domestic work and child care can't be spent on investment in human capital or on paid work. There is also an emotional toll as well. Women who work in paid positions are exhausted because they still have the obligation to do domestic labor, which Arlie Hochschild has called the "second shift."[49] In modern societies, women's entry into the workforce was not accompanied by a corresponding decrease in household labor.

The link between paid labor and the domestic division of labor isn't the only distinctive aspect of gender inequality. A number of sociologists have argued that differences between men and women in social behavior may be due to biological differences. In one much debated article, Richard Udry argues that stereotypically female behavior is due to the mother's hormonal levels during pregnancy.[50] That is, mothers with high testosterone levels during pregnancy are less likely to have children who grow up and exhibit "feminine" behavior. This correlation suggested to Udry that the behaviors and attitudes associated with differences between men and women aren't due solely to socialization but also to social environments that affect physical development.

A question that remains, though, is how theory can explain the unusual pattern of inequality associated with gender—how women can lag behind in many areas yet succeed in others. Here, I appeal to a series of arguments offered by Cecilia Ridgeway to explain this pattern.[51] Hers is not the only argument that has been offered, but it is instructive in that it is general in scope and relies on mechanisms that are typically found in the new theory of inequality. Ridgeway suggests that gender is one of the primary ways that people frame each other in interactions. Gender is fundamental. Once a person has been viewed as male or female in a social situation, he or she is treated in different ways that are hard to shake. Ridgeway, however, argues that this framing interacts with context. The way gender informs interactions varies greatly from situation to situation. The world of the high-tech start-up is vastly different than the classroom. Empirically, these contexts seem to affect how people view men and women. In more structured and bureaucratic contexts, people in general seem to be willing to assign values of leadership and competency to women, which explains why women can achieve parity in education but not in less-structured areas such as high tech.

This sort of argument shares much with older arguments about gender, especially those that claim that gender is built into social institutions. R. W. Connell's argument about gender in politics makes exactly this claim.[52] In a number of books, Connell argues that states rely on masculinity to justify themselves, inform law and policy, and treat their citizens. Thus, gender is interwoven with the state from areas such as leadership to areas such as reproductive rights and labor law. Newer arguments, however, such as Ridgeway's, draw attention to the tacit understandings of gender instead of to explicit ascriptions. By shifting the terms of debate over gender from issues such as essentialism (i.e., Is there an intrinsic, nonsocially defined dimension of gender?) to framings (i.e., How do people's beliefs about the world inform their interactions with men and women?), this type of theory is capable of producing mechanisms that are suited for explaining the subtle variation in differences between men and women that are observed across different social contexts.

In a separate article, Ridgeway provides an important conceptual link between social status and inequality that summarizes a great deal of contemporary thinking. The main argument is that social status results in widely held beliefs about the validity of certain groups, which then results in specific groups receiving disproportionate access to resources.[53] Paralleling some of Bonilla-Silva's arguments about the link between racial attitudes and institutional racism, Ridgeway makes a very general argument about the path from status to inequality. This argument is especially important for modern sociology because it connects the institutions we use to organize our lives (firms, schools, etc.) with the attitudes and dispositions (the habitus) that drive inequality in social interaction and decision making.

SOCIAL POWER: A MODERN TRADITION

So far in this chapter, I have discussed inequality in reference to a number of important theoretical innovations, such as intersectionality and habitus theory. In doing so, I have depicted a relatively direct transition from older sociological accounts of inequality that focus on overt social power to accounts that focus on subconscious habitus. The mechanisms appearing in studies of inequality have shifted from rather direct forms of coercion—for example, Jim Crow in the American South—to subconscious bundles of attitudes, such as those described by Lareau and Bonilla-Silva. But sociologists remain acutely interested in more traditional accounts of power. In these accounts, sociologists try to describe or illuminate how a person or group of people is able to assert his or her or its interest or will in the world and, most crucially, even over others' objections and resistance. Thus, power is, as Gianfranco Poggi notes, an asymmetrical thing and inherently a sign or creator of inequality.[54] This section reviews the types of explanations offered in this tradition.

What underlies many accounts of inequality is a basic psychological argument. A fundamental feature of humanity is its desire to assert its will in the world. This is obvious when we consider all the ways that people have changed the physical world. The same is true of people's social, economic, and political affairs. States are nothing but entities designed to use the force of law to impose some order and rules within a territory. Markets are full of attempts to place order and structure on the ever-changing constellation of buyers and sellers. In fact, it would be remarkable to have a human society without exercise of power.

Contemporary writers on social power often describe all the different types of power and how they relate to each other. For example, Poggi suggests that power associated with one thing, such as the state, ideas, or economics, is distinct from the power associated with another thing. The way that religions, for example, exercise their power is different than the way states do it because religions are about socially constructed ideas, whereas states can rely on the police, the military, and other forms of physical coercion. Other students of power try to unravel the many dimensions of a single instance of power. A highly influential book by Steven Lukes, *Power: A Radical View* (1974), argues that power has multiple features. Power may be exercised within a specific instance of decision making, such as legislators passing a new law. Power may also be exercised by shaping interests: legislators might, for example, pass over alternative policies that were not discussed.

Lukes claims that an additional aspect of power lies in the ability to set agendas and control political institutions. In addition to acting on specific policies and expressing preferences by focusing on some policy over others, one may exclude entire groups and set the terms of debate, wherein some policies are not even able to be discussed. *Power: A Radical View* still retains its interest because Lukes's description of social power helps readers develop nuanced understandings of how power is created and exercised in society.

Finally, modern social power theorists discuss the specific location of power. Perhaps the most prominent modern scholar to address this issue is the great humanist Michel Foucault. In a highly influential text, *The History of Sexuality*, Foucault says that power is literally everywhere.[55] Power isn't just what presidents and executives do. Power resides in all relationships. The teacher exerts power over her students, men exert power over women, and so forth. In fact, one might even argue that the power of presidents and executives simply can't exist without these forms of "micropower." The policies of presidents are empty words if the common man refuses to enforce the law and give it meaning. An even more radical argument suggests that it is often the case that political institutions merely formalize what the wider culture already believes to be true. Indeed, in a number of texts Foucault argues that the regulation of sexuality in the West was preceded by a discussion among intellectuals that cast nonheterosexuals as defective, ill, or immoral.[56]

WE DON'T NEED WATCHERS IF WE WATCH OURSELVES

In today's sociology, theories of social power have merged with theories of habitus and inequality. Sociologists who make this theoretical move often, unsurprisingly, rely on a argument that was originally formulated in Foucault's most well-known book, *Discipline and Punish* (1975). In that text, Foucault claims that modern social power does not directly operate through coercion, as it did in earlier eras, when kings would send knights and soldiers to punish deviants and dissidents. Modern social power is instead achieved through self-regulation. That is, people internalize the rules of order because they always suspect that they are being monitored. To illustrate this idea, Foucault uses the example of the "panopticon," an imaginary prison described by philosopher Jeremy Bentham. Foucault argues that it is possible to have an orderly prison if people suspect that they are being constantly watched. In this hypothetical prison, there would be a tower in the middle. The person in the tower can see the prisoners, but the prisoners can't see into the tower, so they don't know if they are being watched. According to this explanation, the mechanism for why people in modern societies are more orderly is that they have internalized the eternal watchman of the panopticon. The metaphor of the panopticon carries great weight among critical social theorists. We now live in a world where all the supermarkets have cameras, as do gas stations and airports. It is also a world where powerful nation-states routinely collect and analyze the population's emails and phone calls. Surveillance is ubiquitous, and self-administered social control is the result.

In sociology, Foucault's self-regulation argument is used to describe how people or groups conform to some sort of system of inequality. For example, sociologists who study the legal academy have found that law schools are extremely sensitive to external rankings and internalize the values that motivate these rankings.[57] Even though law schools insist that it is inappropriate to rank them, law school professors accept the rankings created, for example, by the *US News & World Report* and actively compete for a higher position in them. Because law school professors feel they are constantly judged, they accept the rankings as something real, try to conform to them, and to some degree accept them as legitimate. The *US News & World Report* ranking is a legal panopticon, forcing the legal academy to regulate itself. The broader theory of inequality implicit in this study is that highly quantified systems of status, which are now common in Western nations, have a "reactive" character, wherein people take rankings seriously and change their actions to accommodate themselves to the ranking system.

The internalized "watcher" is also extremely injurious. Believing that one is under constant surveillance can sometimes lead to further inequality. A recent ethnography by Alice Goffman describes how the penal system creates a destabilizing sense of surveillance among young black men.[58] Following a group of young black men from a low-income Philadelphia neighborhood, Goffman chronicles how entanglement with the legal system leads to a crippling amount of surveillance. Once a man has been in prison and is released on parole, everyday life becomes a battle with the state's various punishment mechanisms. Goffman reports that the men she spent time with claimed to avoid hospitals because they feared that the police would routinely search the hospitals' visitor logs to look for individuals with outstanding search warrants. Constant encounters with the police, parole officers, and other agents of the state eventually inculcates the feeling of constant anxiety, which makes it very difficult to reenter the labor market or educational system.

Although field studies such as Goffman's amply document the crippling effects of the prison system on individuals, it is only by taking a large-scale view that one fully appreciates the role that prisons have in hampering African Americans. For example, numerous studies have found that having a criminal record makes it much more difficult for black men to obtain job interviews.[59] Incarceration is also responsible for interrupting the educational careers of young people. Prison time is one of the most important factors used in predicting that an individual will not attend or graduate college, which is one of the de facto pre-requisites for higher-paying jobs. Other studies have shown that incarceration has serious health effects.[60] These effects include stress, higher blood pressure, and earlier mortality. When millions of people are put in prison, it is not hard to appreciate that entire communities will see their human and social capital destroyed on a massive scale. For this reason, it might be said that inequality is enforced through violence. But, in this type of theory, it is not the violence of the lynch mob or the slaveholder. Instead, violence is channeled through the state via a complex system of prisons and police. It is "violence by other means."

• • •

This chapter identified a major shift in the theory of inequality as it is understood within the discipline of sociology. In earlier theory, the mechanisms generating inequality had to do with physical violence, using the power of the state to segregate people and directly tarnishing the image and reputation of low-status groups. One might describe this view as the "overt" approach to social domination. There is nothing subtle about how power is exercised or experienced. The new theory of inequality, reliant on the idea of social fields, situates people in an invisible, complex web of relationships, rules, and norms. These rules have little to do with economic efficiency or society's coordination problems, as might be suggested by other theories described in this book. These rules are the result of power relationships, and they can be further manipulated by those who wish to perpetuate their advantaged status.

Even when modern stratification researchers discuss violence, such as mass incarceration, they note that it relies on an expansive apparatus of social attitudes, legal codes, and administrative procedures that make it look as if violence is not being carried out against low-status groups. The judge who imposes a harsh sentence on an African American defendant in court is not directly punishing that person for his or her ethnicity. The judge is just applying a law, which is written without explicit reference to background, even when there is widespread consensus that it has disproportionate impacts on minorities.

This wave of research ultimately suggests that modern theories of inequality have converged on a "submerged" approach to inequality. By that, I mean that the identity that is under dispute or contention (e.g., gender or social class) is now buried under layers of laws, attitudes, and actions that do not directly reference or express social identity. An ideology of equality requires that inequality be pursued in powerful but indirect ways. Status and social order are coupled, but status is not directly referenced in the language that is used to describe, define, and enforce inequality. In simpler words, when we make our social world, group membership and status go hand in hand, but we establish this relationship in a way so we don't have to talk about it.

3

STRATEGIC ACTION

ACORE finding of education research is that college graduates earn more money than high school graduates, much more money. College graduates on average earn about 80 to 90 percent more than people who have earned only a high school diploma.[1] This sum, called the "college premium," might amount to millions of dollars over the course of one's life.[2] Some postgraduate degrees, such as medicine, are associated with even higher incomes. One might plausibly ask, "If college has such a great economic payoff, then why do many people drop out or not attend at all?"

In previous chapters, I mentioned some explanations for why people might persist in school. There are psychological factors, such as academic ability, and there are social factors, such as family resources or a history of discrimination (see chapter 2). The issue of college enrollment and graduation draws attention to a different type of explanation that sociologists might use to answer this question: a cost–benefit analysis. In other words, sociologists will often ask how people weigh the costs and benefits of an action as they attempt to achieve their goals.

Regarding college graduation and future income, a sociologist would quickly recognize that a college degree does indeed lead to a much higher level of future income.[3] Now, the question is the cost. College, like most serious undertakings, is not without enormous cost. For example, study after study has shown that tuition and fees have increased much faster than inflation, resulting in a situation where a student might easily pay a quarter of a million dollars for four years of course work. Students often acquire even more loans in working toward advanced degrees, such as MDs, PhDs, and MBAs. There are also time costs. College degrees usually take four years to earn, and many students take longer than this to finish. Opportunity costs are also large. A student who goes to college for four years forgoes four years of salary and wages. Finally, there is the issue of the average college premium. Many college graduates will earn less than the average college premium. The student who earns a bachelor's degree in drama and works in theater is unlikely to obtain the same return on his investment as the student who earns a degree in engineering.[4] The payoff for some degrees simply isn't that large.

By tallying these costs, one is drawn to the conclusion that college is not a uniformly wise choice for all students. For example, the student who has strong academic skills, ample family resources, and a taste for science can readily acquire an engineering degree that will in all likelihood result in a much higher income, thus justifying the costs and risk of college. In contrast, a hypothetical drama student might guess that, given what actors usually make, it might be wise to drop out and just start working in the performing arts. He may not earn much in income, but at least he has not paid tens of thousands or even hundreds of thousands of dollars for a college degree. Similarly, a student with very weak academic skills might justifiably accept the fact that it might be very hard to earn a college degree and that dropping out after matriculation would leave her with onerous student loans. Thus, we have obtained some explanations for why a significant number of students don't enroll in college or complete their degree even when there is a large income boost associated with a college degree.

The sort of explanation I just offered is very different than the types of explanations I offered about education in earlier chapters. In previous chapters, the analytical focus was on collective or group processes. Chapter 2, on power and hierarchies, describes how people achieve status by linking group membership with certain resources. In contrast, the analysis of college completion here relies mainly on the perceived costs and benefits. The explanation is individualistic in character, and for the most part it doesn't rely on the characteristics of groups.

This chapter explores the arguments that sociologists make when they consider how individuals weigh the costs and benefits of their actions. The example of the student who weighs the benefits of a college degree is a textbook illustration of "rational-choice theory," a theory that relies on the tools of economics to explain behavior. In addition to unpacking the basic ideas of rational-choice theory, this chapter investigates how sociologists have expanded the classical rational-choice framework. The main insight is that sociologists have a very broad idea of what counts as a resource that can be used to achieve one's goals. More so than scholars in fields such as economics and political science, sociologists consider how personal relationships and group context factor into individual choices. Thus, the different examples found in this chapter are variations on the theme of how social context affects choice or how social relationships advance goals.

This chapter presents the different theories of resources and choice that are commonly found in sociology. I present them in an order that emphasizes how they grew out of the basic framework of rational-choice theory. Thus, I start with rational-choice theory itself and briefly explain the theory's premises and modes of explanation. Then I discuss how mechanisms appear in rational-choice theory. The remainder of the chapter addresses three different avenues of theoretical development. I call the first "sociological rational choice" because it focuses on the types of mechanisms that are common throughout sociology—the role of human relationships in guiding action and the importance of groups. The second type of theory, "bounded-rationality theory," is found in sociology and related fields such as management and political science that frequently address decision making in group contexts. Instead of adding relationships to rational-choice models, theorists in this tradition modify rational choice in ways that account for how social contexts can make decision making very challenging and difficult. I then discuss a third type of theory that uses sociological ideas to modify ideas in economics. From time to time, economists will use insights from sociology to enrich and expand their explanations of traditional economic research. By comparing the different types of theory that emerged from classical rational-choice theory, one can better appreciate how sociology and other fields contribute to our understanding of how people make strategic choices.

RATIONAL-CHOICE THEORY

Sociologists have long been interested in cost–benefit analysis. For example, in the mid–twentieth century, social exchange theory enjoyed popularity within sociology. Developed by George Homans, social exchange theory focused on rewards and positive reinforcement.[5] People would continue to act in the same way if they received some positive benefit. For example, the student obeys the teacher as long as the teacher rewards the student. Although popular in sociology, social exchange theory was eventually replaced by rational-choice theory as the standard model of how people judge costs and benefits.[6] Both theories share much in common, but rational-choice theory is formulated in a way that makes it very general and thus suited to a wide range of problems in sociology and other fields.

The fundamental assumption of rational-choice theory is that people should be understood as actors who are trying to maximize their utility. It is important to note that utility is an undefined "primitive" concept in rational-choice theory. It is also important to note that utility refers only to "usefulness," not to happiness. I go to bankruptcy court to resolve my debt not because it makes me happy but because it is better than the alternatives. Thus, bankruptcy has more "utility" than trying to service extremely large loans. According to rational-choice theory, large-scale phenomena such as institutions or social trends are the outcome of individual utility maximization. Social trends reflect a mass of individuals who are trying to achieve the best alternative available to them. When people decide to riot, it is an expression of an individual calculus. When people set up legal rules or informal norms, they are choosing to follow the rules because it benefits them.[7] This model of human behavior is associated with the discipline of economics, but it can be found in nearly every field where human behavior is analyzed.

Modern rational-choice theory has roots in the seventeenth century and earlier, but two developments in the twentieth century made it possible for this theory to assert itself in disciplines outside of economics. First, in the 1940s the economist Paul Samuelson developed a very simple but very general mathematical framework for utility maximization.[8] In this framework, an individual can be described by his or her preferences. Any preference can be expressed as a numerical function, U, called the "utility function." If I prefer living in New York rather than San Francisco, then

U(New York) is greater than U(San Francisco). According to the assigned values, U(New York) = 3 and U(San Francisco) = 2. The specific numbers don't matter as long as the basic underlying preference order is maintained. If the utility function (U) satisfies some plausible technical conditions, then one can use calculus and other mathematical tools to predict behavior by calculating the utility-optimizing strategy. Because preferences are stated in terms of mathematical functions that can be readily modified, Samuelson's theory provides an intuitive and flexible foundation for economic analysis that can be applied to a wide range of situations.

Second, in the 1960s Gary Becker and other economists made a simple but far-reaching argument: economic analysis can be applied to any social behavior because the consequences of any action can be ranked.[9] Therefore, the logic of cost–benefit analysis need not be limited to financial issues such as taxes, jobs, and the like and can also be applied to topics such as marriage, voting, and crime. At first, Becker's "neoclassical" argument was met with skepticism because noncommercial situations were thought to be outside the realm of economic analysis. However, his arguments gained more credibility as a generation of social scientists began applying cost–benefit analysis to a wide range of social behaviors.[10] Although by no means fully accepted by scholars, cost–benefit analysis remains a common tool for social science.

The impact of the rational-choice argument and others like it has been profound. For example, political scientists are now familiar with Duncan Black's "median-voter theorem" that models voters' preferences and politicians' behavior.[11] According to the model, each voter is represented by a single number x, indicating the policy she wants, and the voter will support the politician who comes closest to giving her what she wants. If the voter wants a 25 percent income tax, and Mitt Romney promises a 30 percent tax, but Barack Obama promises a 35 percent tax, then the voter will support Romney. Thus, in an election with two candidates, it is rational for each candidate to offer a policy that represents the median voter who evenly splits the electorate, with half the voters to the left or the right of the median. To do otherwise allows the other candidate to gain more than 50 percent of the votes by moving more to the left or right of the voter distribution. The median-voter theorem makes no claims about voter intentions, politician motivations, or any aspect of society other than the distribution of voter preferences. Once the median voter's preference is known, then one knows how politicians will behave. Because of its intuitive appeal and straightforward argument, the median-voter theorem has become one of the most discussed and debated ideas in political science.

MECHANISMS

Now that we have explored some classical examples of rational-choice theory, we can ask about mechanisms. What are the X and Y of the typical rational-choice explanation? How does one move from X to Y? In general, the X of a rational-choice explanation is the preference of the people who are being studied. The Y is usually their final choice. For example, one can safely assume that the goal of most corporations is to make money. However, many fail to do so. Corporations lose money, and many will go bankrupt and disappear. Thus, we need an additional process that links people's wants or desires, their final actions, and the consequences of those actions.

The mechanisms that get a person from X to Y in rational-choice theory vary, but there are a few types. Many rational-choice theories appeal to budgets to inform their explanations. I might want to eat at the best restaurant in my town, but I might not have the funds. The limits of the human mind are another mechanism. I may be uncertain about the future, or I may not completely understand all my options, or I may not be able to gather all the information I might need. All of these mechanisms affect my actions. With different information, I might have gone to a different college, for example.

Social conditions and institutional arrangements (e.g., the legal rules for divorce) are another type of mechanism. Probably the most important social condition affecting the translation of choice into action in economic explanations is competition. If I have the only sushi bar in my town, then I can invest my profits differently than if I am competing against other sushi bars. As the owner of the only sushi bar, I can invest in additional locations. If I am competing against others, however, I might think that new locations will most likely not make money, so I invest my profits in other businesses.

The different mechanisms in choice theories dictate further theoretical development. For example, one can apply the basic rational-choice model to any social situation and focus on perceived costs. The next section reviews one well-known study that looks at how college attendance and completion might be affected by people's belief in the likelihood of success and the penalties for failure. Alternatively, one might focus on how social situations complicate decisions. Bounded-rationality theory was developed precisely to address this issue and is very popular among scholars who wish to investigate how managers make choices in large firms and highly competitive markets. Another theoretical alternative is to focus on how people use social contexts to pursue their goals. In other words, one might think about how relationships, customs, and norms facilitate or impede social action. This is the core insight of the "sociological" rational-choice theory discussed later in this chapter. Finally, one might rely on a more traditional version of rational-choice theory but also ask how social contexts determine our preferences, which is what some economists are exploring as they assimilate the insights from other fields.

CHOOSING YOUR EDUCATION

To understand how cost–benefit analysis has evolved in sociology, it helps to begin with an example that is a straightforward application of rational-choice theory. Once again, education provides us with an instructive example. In a highly cited article, "Explaining Educational Differentials" (1997), Richard Breen and John H. Goldthorpe ask why children from differing social backgrounds achieve varying levels of education. Numerous studies have found that children from working-class backgrounds are less likely to enter and complete college, even accounting for academic skills.[12] With a few exceptions, class-based differences in schooling have persisted, even as spending on schools has increased in nearly every industrialized nation over the course of the twentieth century.[13]

To answer their question, Breen and Goldthorpe offer a classical rational-choice explanation: children from working- and middle-class families face substantially different incentives. In other words, college education does not have identical pay-offs for all people. The main argument is that what people get in return from their college education depends on their economic background. The failure to complete a college education for a child from well-off parents has vastly different consequences than it does for the working-class student. The working-class student might be highly encumbered by debt and might return to a less-desirable working-class occupation. In contrast, the child of well-off parents might be insulated from college failure. A wealthy parent can provide "cushioning" for the college dropout.

The model of school completion is intuitive. A child in school is faced with three possible outcomes: leave, remain but fail school, or remain and pass school. Each outcome has a probability of leading to either a less-desirable working-class job or a more desirable, skilled service-sector job. The decision to remain in school is tied to the subjective perception of success, the costs associated with schooling, and the relative benefits of working-class and service-sector jobs. These perceptions vary according to social class. Therefore, the theory produces a parsimonious explanation of educational attainment that can be tested. Educational differences persist when there are relative differences among expectations of school success among working class and middle class parents and children. At the very least, people will pursue a level of education that leaves them as well off as their parents.

It is important to contrast this explanation with those offered by earlier theories of school success. For many years, sociologists thought that factors such as academic performance, cognitive abilities, and family social status determined whether a person completes high school or goes to college.[14] The long-standing story in educational attainment research focuses on abilities and aspirations as the primary mechanism.[15] Educational achievements flow from attitudes, which are shaped by peer and family interactions. Students from more-affluent families adopt their parents' preferences. They want a higher level of education because their parents have presented it as a desirable outcome. Furthermore, as discussed in chapter 2, it is often thought that more-educated parents are more able to guide their children through the educational process.

Breen and Goldthorpe's theory is consistent with some of these ideas. Parents may take academic skills and cognitive abilities into account in determining their children's chance of success. However, Breen and Goldthorpe are quite adamant in insisting that the theory makes no assumptions about different class cultures, as might be assumed by researchers following in Bourdieu's footsteps. It is not assumed that working-class parents care less about schooling than middle-class professional parents or that working-class parents don't know how to game the educational system. It is assumed that all people care about education. What varies is the perceived chance of success and its payoff, which does vary by social class. Everyone cares about education, but some people face different costs for poor academic work.

It is worth discussing the research that followed Breen and Goldthorpe's. Many researchers asked if it is true that perceived chances of success are truly correlated with continuing school. In many cases, it was found to be true.[16] However, other elements of the model did not seem to hold in empirical tests. Studies such as Annette Lareau's field observation of parents (chapter 2) indicate that not all parents have adequate knowledge of schools, so it is hard to ascribe their behavior to explicit cost–benefit calculations. It has also been found that rational-choice models of schooling are often supported by data on aggregate trends in school choices but not by data in models of individual-level school choice.[17] Tabulating educational differences in perceived success, achievement, and class background does conform with rational-choice predictions, but statistical models matching individual beliefs with performance do not. This difference suggests that rational-action theories do succeed in capturing the constraints facing entire categories of people, such as working-class families, but leave much to be desired in explaining individual differences in schooling.

Research on college education highlights the strengths and weaknesses of classical rational-choice sociology. A consistent finding is that perceived chances for success are associated with different choices. Another consistent finding is that tuition and other financial factors, such as financial aid, do influence college attendance and completion. At the same time, some phenomena are not well captured by rational-choice models. Although perceived chances at success matter, the perceived importance of education does not. Apparently everybody thinks education is important. Therefore, beliefs about education's importance don't predict college attendance, even when controlling for other factors. Another issue is how people's desire to complete college is shaped by the educational process itself. A number of studies that examine students from working-class backgrounds find that entering college does not automatically lead to graduation. Rather, as noted in chapter 2, working-class students often lack the "habitus" that would help them get the most out of their education. Thus, issues of identity and interaction with institutions are not easily described by rational-choice models.

SOCIAL CAPITAL THEORY: BETWEEN OVER- AND UNDERSOCIALIZED

In traditional rational-choice theories, individuals act in an "atomistic" fashion. Given a choice, they use their own internal preferences to choose a strategy, a sequence of actions that optimizes their expected utility. The crucial insight is that strategies take into account perceived costs. In Breen and Goldthorpe's study, it is only assumed that people consider the costs and benefits of college and that wealthier students face different risks than less-wealthy students. Many sociologists have realized, however, that group contexts can affect how these strategies are pursued. People incorporate others' ideas and preferences into their own decisions. This may happen explicitly (e.g., a spouse thinking about what a partner wants) or tacitly (e.g., people adopting their ethnic group's views).

This observation represents one of the first important breaks with classical rational-choice theory. The key argument is to be found in Mark Granovetter's analysis of job-search strategies, *Getting a Job: A Study of Contacts and Careers* (1974). He contrasted a classical rational-choice approach to jobs with a more structural view. In the traditional economic model, people obtain a list of jobs and then work through them according to a rule that optimizes the chance of finding a suitable employer. Granovetter's alternative approach also assumes that people are instrumental and seek good jobs. However, Granovetter noticed that people don't always approach the job market as described in this thumbnail sketch. Rarely do people systematically find a list of jobs and rationally sort them. They instead rely on personal networks. They ask their friends, family, and coworkers about the jobs that might exist. This is important for many reasons. Jobs may not be publically advertised. Jobs may have traits that aren't observed from advertisements. Personal referral may lead to more job offers than do cold calls. Thus, personal networks are both a resource and a constraint in job search. They are a resource because personal relationships can lead to information and to jobs. They are a constraint because a person who does not possess the right types of relationships may be at a disadvantage compared to the person who knows people who know about jobs.

At first, Granovetter's observation about job searches may seem trivial, but it is not. The important element of his observation is that social relationships constrain and influence seemingly impersonal economic calculations. Furthermore, recognizing the importance of networks, Granovetter made a vivid and original argument: casual acquaintances may matter more than strong friends because strong friends already know what you know. Casual acquaintances connect a person to new groups of people and new job opportunities. He called this connection the "strength of weak ties." This theory combines the idea that people rationally pursue interests and the idea that a person's social environment can affect how these goals are achieved.

Following Granovetter, a number of other sociologists developed new theories of social resources. A very famous example is James Coleman's social capital theory, introduced in the late 1980s. He argued that group characteristics can help individuals achieve their goals. He called such group characteristics "social capital."[18] One example is trust within an ethnic group. An ethnic group that develops a strong sense of social solidarity allows its members to act in ways that confer concrete economic advantages. Coleman used the case of Jewish diamond merchants to demonstrate his theory. A key issue in the diamond trade is that the price depends on the precise assessment of a gem's flaws and imperfections. A buyer needs to take possession of a diamond and examine it for a long period of time. Coleman noted that Jewish diamond merchants trust each other because of their backgrounds. They are much more likely to entrust each other with expensive and easy-to-steal diamonds, which reduces transaction costs and facilitates trade.

Coleman's other example is "social closure." A group exhibits social closure if there are many closed "loops." If person A knows person B, and B knows C, then A will also know C. Loops are important because information will cycle quickly through the group. For instance, B learns something, so it will eventually be learned by person A even if A doesn't not hear about it from B. Coleman argued that social closure may be beneficial to individuals because they can learn of important information. His example was schooling. He argued that schools in socially closed communities would yield better outcomes because parents would quickly learn about discipline problems. Even if the schoolteachers didn't report to a specific parent, other parents might mention the problem. Coleman used this sort of reasoning to explain why Catholic schools often have better student outcomes than public schools. Parents can indirectly monitor and control their children by using information obtained from other members of their religious group who have children in the same school. Public-school parents may not have access to a similar network of parents and teachers.

Since these early formulations, social capital theory has been expanded. An important development is the study of variation in social capital. Much in the same way that an economist may explain economic development by reference to technological or financial capital, many sociologists have argued that social capital can explain why some nations are wealthier than others. A high level of trust in society may allow entrepreneurs to hire people so they can run growing businesses. Similarly, trust between workers and owners can be helpful if owners need to temporarily cut wages in a recession. A lack of trust means that workers may not allow the owners to renegotiate contracts, which may thus jeopardize the firm.[19]

A very interesting application of social capital has been in studies of ethnic groups. A number of researchers have noted that that there are marked differences between ethnic groups in terms of their income and their internal social organization. For example, African Americans, compared to other American groups, have a much lower rate of entrepreneurship. Asian Americans have a very high rate of business ownership, which often depends on recruiting kin and friends into family businesses.[20] Recent studies have focused on the social capital found in urban areas. A study by urban sociologist Mario Small finds that public-service agencies act as places where the urban poor make vital connections to organizations, such as child-care groups, that can help them.[21]

In reviewing social capital studies, it is important to emphasize that they make no normative statements. Like money, social capital is merely a resource that can be used for any purpose, a point Coleman made in his original article on the topic. Highly risky criminal behavior is made possible by the sort of trust associated with ethnic groups. Criminal gangs are often based on shared ethnicity for precisely that reason. Similarly, white-collar crime is also facilitated by social ties and group trust. Consider the recent Madoff scandal, where professional money manager Bernie Madoff set up a years-long pyramid scheme that stole billions of dollars from investors. Committing one of the largest instances of financial fraud in American history, Madoff took millions of dollars in client money and did not invest it. He instead used the funds to pay a previous round of clients. The remarkable thing is not that someone wished to enrich himself through deceit but rather that the deceit was made possible by that person's use of social capital.[22] Madoff and his associates recruited investors through personal ties and shared ethnic background. The pressure was enough to overwhelm skeptics who were suspicious of Madoff's incredible profits. The Madoff scheme is a sobering reminder that social capital is a neutral resource that can be used for good or bad ends.

STRUCTURAL HOLES AND SOCIAL SKILL

A very interesting example of rational action under social constraints is Ron Burt's structural-holes theory.[23] Ron Burt starts with a basic observation about group life. We are often divided into multiple groups with few overlaps. In academia, for example, mathematics and chemistry professors work in different departments and have few professional interactions. Within a firm, workers who do different jobs or who have different ranks may not interact very much. A consequence of social division is that there are opportunities for arbitrage. In other words, each group has its own resources, and there is much redundancy. Mathematics professors will talk only about math with each other, and chemists do the same. But that also means there are chances to combine resources by linking groups. It might be possible, for example, for a mathematician to create a field of "mathematical chemistry" by talking to chemists and combining ideas. This field would be new because mathematicians and chemists don't normally talk to each other very much. Ron Burt calls the gap between groups "structural holes," and his theory is that people who are "near" structural holes have the potential to advance themselves by bridging these holes. In other words, if a person is in some way between groups, he or she has more knowledge that can be strategically used.

The theory of structural holes is attractive to many social scientists because it addresses a common feature of social life. People split into groups, and those who connect separate groups can benefit greatly from making the connection. An example from my own research in political sociology illustrates this point well. Scholars have observed that a successful protest group needs to link different kinds of people because most political issues have narrow constituencies. A protest to save the whales may not appeal to labor union members, but the environmentalists may need union members to boost the size of the protest and increase the visibility of their cause. To address this problem, many political movements will create "hybrid activist organizations" that are designed to link different groups, such as environmentalists and union members. It is not hard to imagine a group called "Labor Saves the Whales" that encourages working-class people to save the environment. Analysis of data on political organizations collected by my research partner (Michael T. Heaney) and I shows that such hybrid organizations attract more members and are more central in the movement's social networks. Thus, in politics, it pays to bridge a structural hole.[24]

Burt's theory has a highly intuitive formalization. In network analysis, it is common to represent a relationship with a line between two people. For example, if A is friends with B, then that friendship is visualized by the configuration "A–B." Mathematically, a network can be presented as a matrix of zeros and ones. If A and B are linked, then the spot corresponding to A–B is filled in with a one. If A and B are not linked, then the spot is filled with a zero.

Within this matrix, it is easy to describe two groups, X and Y, who are separate from each other and thus represent a structural hole. In the matrix, there are "blocks" of ones that represent each group. Blocks of zeros represent the lack of ties. The interesting empirical finding is that an individual's distance to the holes (that is, the blocks of zeros,) is statistically correlated with income and the potential to come up with innovative ideas. In other words, the structure of relationships is a resource for personal wealth and economic development.[25]

Although Burt and most researchers do find evidence that structural holes and other forms of social capital correlate with successful social action, there are important exceptions and cases where the story is more complicated. Burt looks at one such example in an article that analyzed the careers of three thousand employees at a large corporation.[26] He obtained data on their social ties in the firm, which allowed him to test the hypothesis that people who are in loosely connected parts of the networks have more career opportunities. For men, this was the case. Those men with many structural holes experienced more promotion at work, indicating that men succeed when they bridge gaps. In contrast, women displayed the opposite correlation. Women are more likely to be promoted if they are located in more dense parts of the firm's network that have fewer structural holes. Burt's explanation is that women who are promoted faster tend to come from networks that are concentrated around specific individuals (i.e., the person is a "hub" in the network). He also finds that the networks around female executives tend to have more "span"; in other words, they reach farther. This finding suggests to Burt that women are more likely than men to rely on sponsored mobility— they are successful because they "borrow" the social capital of nearby network "elites." Further, it suggests that there is a problem with gender in that firm. The need to "borrow" social capital indicates that the borrower is an outsider. Thus, if policy is meant to create equity between men and women, then it has to consider how to alleviate this problem.

Burt's theory of structural holes points to an even deeper issue in sociology. The classical economic model of human action depicts a person who processes information and judges outcomes. James Coleman's and Ron Burt's theories add to this view. Their work depicts humans as manipulating their social world in the service of their personal goals. They create trust, exploit friendship, and bridge groups. These actions are defined in terms of their social world. This observation motivates Neil Fligstein's theory of social skill.[27] According to Fligstein, social skill is an individual's ability to manipulate or otherwise exploit his or her social environment, which is described in institutionalist terms (e.g., norms or cognitive schema that regulate individuals and organizations). Institutional logics motivate behavior in markets or in nonprofit situations. Network ties link the various actors in a social field. Actors use implicit and tacit knowledge to promote their goals within the workplace.

The essence of Fligstein's argument is that individuals vary in their ability to exploit these features of the social world. For example, numerous historians have noted that Lyndon Johnson was often an effective political leader because he possessed an intimate knowledge of how the U.S. Senate worked.[28] Numerous biographical studies of business leaders show that they often have a deeply ingrained knowledge of the business field that they have transformed. Steve Jobs, for example, had worked for a prominent research lab at Stanford University before entering college. Mark Zuckerberg received computer-programming lessons as an adolescent and then formed close ties with friends who attended leading technical schools such as Cal Tech. By the time he entered college, he had years of programming experience and close associations with people who knew a great deal about the world of consumer electronics and the Internet. Both Jobs and Zuckerberg at early ages acquired not only the technical skills needed to help design new consumer products but also the social skill needed to navigate the social field of Silicon Valley.[29] "Social skill" is an umbrella idea that brings together the many ways individuals exploit and shape their social environment in the pursuit of their goals. For that reason, it brings attention to mechanisms that link individual goals, social environments, and outcomes.

BOUNDED RATIONALITY AND BEYOND

The previous two sections have discussed the incorporation of social structure into theories of strategic action. In this section, I would like to discuss an alternative path of theoretical development—bounded rationality and garbage-can theory. As noted earlier, one problem with traditional rational-choice theory is that it assumes actors live in a world where it easy to evaluate alternatives. This assumption is problematic. In practice, choices may be too numerous or difficult to evaluate. There may not be well-defined alternatives. This intuitive observation led to the social theory developed by Herb Simon, James March, and the "Carnegie school" of organizational research.

Simon, March, and their followers assumed that rational choice, as originally stated in economics, is difficult for "real-world" actors to implement. Take an example from sociologist Michel Crozier, who studied how firms reach decisions.[30] According to a classic rational-choice model, a firm that needs to buy a building would first look at all available buildings and then estimate the value of each building. Even in a small town, this task would be unnecessarily onerous. What firms do instead is engage in a limited search for something that is "good enough." This modification of rational choice, from optimization to "satisficing," is a key theoretical moment that allowed social scientists to retain rational-choice theory's focus on goal seeking while dropping the need to precisely specify the best option.

The move to bounded rationality motivated a new style of social science wherein researchers could describe people behaving in complex environments. For example, admitting that people might have limited rationality allowed March and Simon to describe the internal workings of firms.[31] Managers simply can't monitor all employees or foresee the situations that an organization must deal with. Instead, they must cede authority to others or develop routines and procedures that are meant to force employees to follow certain rules. Thus, firms break up into subgroups, and the subgroups are governed by rules and procedures, not by the CEO's daily edict.

Perhaps the most radical implication of bounded rationality is a theory called "garbage-can theory." Developed in the early 1970s by James March, Michael D. Cohen, and Johan Olsen,[32] garbage-can theory tries to model situations where the environment is ambiguous and roles are flexible. Take, for example, political decision making. As noted earlier, political actors are often reactive. They can't foresee the problems that may arise. They might not even understand the possible range of problems—How many American officials on September 10, 2011, had any idea of what was to happen the next day? March, Cohen, and Olsen note that these situations are laden with great ambiguity. Who is responsible for combating terrorism? The Department of Defense? The CIA? The Department of State? Should terrorism be combated with a land invasion of another country? With spying? Drone strikes? Terrorism is a vague and broad problem that might be addressed in many ways.

The way to analyze this situation is to avoid saying, "These are the choices, and this is how each person values them." One should instead focus on the "stream" of problems, people, and solutions. In the federal government, officers hold meetings where various people might or might not show up. The agenda of the meetings is shaped by an odd parade of events. Some may be predictable (next week's election), whereas other may be inherently unpredictable (a coup in a foreign country). The final decision that emerges from a meeting on terrorism depends on who shows up, what they care about, and what tools they have. If the CIA representative appears, the "solution" to terrorism will reflect the CIA's interests—perhaps the development of a more extensive spying apparatus. If the meeting happens to be dominated by officials from the Department of Defense, then perhaps the "solution" will involve boots on the ground.

Like battling ghosts in the film *Ghostbusters* (1984), organizational life is about "crossing the streams." In a massive, complex organization such as the federal government, it is hard to argue that a single person sits down and decides policy. Policy instead emerges when a problem appears and certain people with certain tools happen to be paying attention. This model, where random people and problems are tossed together, is called "garbage-can theory." Its name uses an apt metaphor because in daily life people randomly throw different items into the garbage can. Cohen, March, and Olsen explain: "one can view a choice opportunity as a garbage can into which various kinds of problems and solutions are dumped by participants as they are generated."[33]

What is important about garbage-can theory for this book is that it represents one way of addressing an important criticism of rational-choice theory. Rather than assume high-information actors in rather simple situations, we assume actors with bounded rationality who are randomly brought together to resolve challenging situations.

HOW ECONOMISTS DEAL WITH THESE ISSUES

This book is about how sociologists develop their theories, so this section briefly departs from that overall goal by looking at how economists have dealt with issues that have arisen in rational-choice research. In addition to being intrinsically interesting, examining the economic response to the strengths and weaknesses of rational-choice theory allows us to see an alternative path of theoretical development. Although there is a vibrant tradition of heterodox economics that rejects rational-choice theory, economists have generally tried to account for identity and social structure by modifying the theory's basic framework. Take, for example, recent work by George Akerlof and Rachel Kranton.[34] They begin with a very basic sociological observation: people identify themselves with a group, and this identity guides their action. People may see themselves as part of an ethnic group or a gender or an economic class (e.g., workers). Casual observation leads to more examples. People identify with religions, consumer groups (e.g., Mac users), political parties, youth subcultures (e.g., Goths), and many other types of groups.

Akerlof and Kranton argue that economists should look at how social identities determine utility functions. An individual's group membership should affect how he or she values things, which will then be factored into how economists explain social behavior. A simple example: ethnicity and television viewing. Marketers know well that there are large and obvious differences in consumption by various ethnic groups. Television viewing is one well-known instance. With the exception of sports, there is little ethnic-group overlap in the list of the most-watched American television shows. Black viewers watch shows that attract very small white audiences. Because people want to see shows that feature characters like themselves, there are large differences in the popularity of television shows across ethnic groups.

Black–white differences in television viewing may be an interesting fact for marketers, but the link between group identity and behavior also has broader implications for economics and social theory more generally. If it is the case that group identity is a pervasive and important feature of the social world, then all rational-choice analysis should consider how these identities factor into strategic behaviors. Akerlof and Kranton use the example of schools.[35] As sociologists and education researchers have documented, there are distinct subcultures in schools. Some students focus on academics, whereas others focus on sports. There are cultural subgroups as well, whose members identify with particular music scenes or consumer goods. Akerlof and Kranton argue that group identity is associated with academic performance. Those who adopt the academic identity have on average better grades than those whose identity is based on other issues. The authors use this connection to explain the puzzling fact that schools with

similar resources often produce widely divergent outcomes—
students vary in how much they identify with academics. Another
example these authors provide is work effort.[36] A fundamental
issue in management is how to get employees to accomplish their
tasks. Managers are often advised to implement a system of material rewards and punishments. Akerlof and Kranton argue that
identity is an important factor affecting how much effort people
put into their job. To elicit greater effort, it is not enough simply to alter the incentives for workers. The manager must instead
align the workers' identity with the organization.

In response to the need to account for social identity, Akerlof
and Kranton modified the basic rational-choice framework.
People still have well-defined choices, and they can easily assign
values to possible outcomes, but now group identity affects how
people assign value. The theoretical difference between Akerlof
and Kranton and other economists, such as Gary Becker, or even
rational-choice sociologists, such as Breen and Goldthorpe, is
that Akerlof and Kranton readily admit that people are fundamentally different. In the jargon of modern economics, the world
is full of heterogeneous agents. The situation isn't one in which
we all prefer the same thing (e.g., money) but face different constraints. People really are different from each other. You can't
make white viewers watch television shows geared to black audiences by decreasing cable television subscription prices and thus
making the shows more accessible. Blacks and whites may simply
want different forms of entertainment.

The other major departure from rational-choice theory is
behavioral economics. The motivating observation of behavioral
economics is that people possess biases in how they perceive costs
and benefits. For example, experiments consistently show that
people can't accurately estimate risk. They will overestimate or
underestimate things such as the chance of winning the lottery.
This finding is usually established in experimental settings where

subjects are required to compute the average payout of a game. Analysis of the experimental data will typically show that the subjects consistently got the answer wrong.[37]

The major innovation of behavioral economics, aside from documenting all type of human error, is to factor these biases into existing rational-choice models. In predicting how people behave, economists must model how people weigh uncertain events. Thus, a bias requires a modification to the subjective probability that people assign to events, such as winning the lottery or completing college. The latter is an example of how the processes that interest sociologists are now explored in the discipline of economics. Having a low level of education, for example, might lead to more systematic biases in knowledge and decision making.

These two examples of how economists have responded to the limits of traditional rational-choice models show the alternative paths taken by sociology and economics. In general, economists prefer to leave the basic framework of rational-choice theory untouched. Akerlof and Kranton's modification is that there are simply different types of actors. Behavioral economics assumes uniform actors but takes social differences into account by modifying the perceived probabilities of expected outcomes. In contrast, sociologists have focused on how individuals exploit social structure (e.g., social capital theory and structural-holes theory) or how the environment constrains individuals and imposes costs (e.g., weak-ties theory).

CRITICISMS OF RATIONAL CHOICE AND RELATED IDEAS IN SOCIOLOGY

Strategic theories of social behavior are the subject of much debate within sociology. It is worth mentioning the criticisms of rational-choice theory, especially those commonly made by sociologists. My view is that some criticisms are easily answered, whereas others draw attention to the genuine limitations of rational-choice theory. For example, many critics have said that rational-choice theory requires too much from an individual.[38] To make a decision, who can possibly do all the mathematical calculations at the center of the theory?[39] This, I think, is one of the more easily answered criticisms. Rational-choice theory doesn't require that the individual perform any difficult computations. Indeed, the more thoughtful applications of the theory depict people with simple utility functions. A person looking for a marriage partner may want someone who is educated or of the same religion. A high school student might strive to be accepted into the college with the highest prestige that will admit him or her. Mathematics is used to study the consequences of the utility function assignment that are not immediately obvious to the people involved. For example, what if everyone decided to look for a spouse with a college degree? Or how many parties can survive in a political system with first-past-the-post voting? A mathematical model can help answer these questions because you can deduce implications that are not immediately clear from the model's assumptions. But the individual in these explanations is not required to perform any complex calculations.

Another criticism is that rational-choice theory assumes that actors have perfect information—that people make judgments with full knowledge of relevant alternatives and their likely consequences.[40] This criticism, too, can be easily addressed. In practice, most rational-choice theory uses the language of probability. If an individual has a reasonable understanding of the choice to be made, she may assign a subjective weight to each option. In assessing the value of a lottery ticket, she may decide, "The chance of my winning is 1 percent, and there is a 99 percent of losing at the lottery." Thus, rational choice has a very standardized and intuitive response. If people can list the available choices, they can assign weights that reflect how much they think any outcome will occur, and they can factor those weights into their final decisions.

The most serious criticisms of rational choice don't focus on technical issues, such as perfect information. They focus on the theory's underlying assumptions. One very important criticism is that human beings don't always make explicit comparisons of alternatives.[41] This issue is important because every rational-choice explanation starts with a description of alternative actions and their values. But people have strongly formed opinions that seem resistant to more information about the value of choices. For example, numerous experiments by political psychologists show that people will often oppose a proposed government policy based on who proposed it (e.g., a Democrat), not on information about the policy itself.[42] In politics, people seem to be responding to automatic intuitive feelings rather than making explicit comparisons of alternatives.

Another criticism is that many social situations are simply difficult to effectively model with an unqualified version of rational-choice theory. For example, it is often noted that preferences may be interdependent. That is, a person's preferences may be changed in response to others' actions. This interdependence is important because reciprocity is common in social life. Although the idea of responding to other people is intuitive, there are multiple ways to model the behavior, and it is not immediately clear which model is best. In a review of the issue, economist Joel Sobel notes that many assumptions of rational choice theory, such as time-stable preferences, need to be relaxed, and more sophisticated models, such as repeated-game models, need to be considered.[43]

Another example of a social process that is hard to model comes from political scientist John Kingdon, who notes that policy is often driven by "windows of opportunity" that are hard to understand ex ante.[44] Kingdon notes that there are many predictable problems that people can foresee and assess alternative courses of action. Elections are an excellent example. Most of the time political leaders know that an election is approaching. They can recruit supporters, raise money, and attack challengers. It makes a great deal of sense to say that there are strategies (e.g., choosing to publicly attack an opponent or to "stay positive"), and people can guess how successful each strategy might be.

In contrast, other events are extremely hard to model in this way. Some events are rare or not properly understood ex ante, so it is hard to say that actors have time to develop strategies beforehand. For example, the president of the United States may not understand the complex risks of an unpredictable earthquake that triggers an explosion at a nuclear reactor in Japan. Or he may not completely understand that a loose network of criminals can occasionally conduct a catastrophic attack on civilians, such as the attacks on September 11, 2001.[45] When these types of events occur, they do two things. First, they force actors to rely on "ready to go" responses ("We must act immediately") rather than careful comparison of alternatives. Second, they open a Pandora's box of action and outcomes. A catastrophic event will draw the attention of the public and policy entrepreneurs, who suddenly enter a policy domain and change its dynamics. Thus, policy may emerge from a complex window of opportunity created by unexpected "catastrophic events" that in the short term produce a wide range of options with unclear consequences that are exploited by a diverse set of political actors. It is difficult to argue that in such a situation people are anticipating problems and making explicit judgments about risk. Describing a utility function that assigns value to an ambiguously defined stream of problems is a great challenge. Kingdon chooses to use the more flexible framework of garbage-can theory to describe this type of situation.

One issue with many theories of choice that merits more discussion is the reification of social categories. In other words, rational-choice models depict people who have clear and stable social identities, and it is tempting to assume that these categories are fixed things. Sociologists know that this assumption cannot always be made. It is common to talk about black–white differences, and we might be tempted to think that ethnic identities are rigid. But this is not true. For example, research on the family shows that people often change their ethnic identification in response to changes in family structure, such as divorce or death of a spouse or other loved one. This is because many people factor their spouse's social identity into their own identity. Once the spouse dies, then people feel free to adjust their identity.[46] The relevance of this fact to this chapter is that rational-choice theories often seem to reify social categories. These sorts of models should instead be thought of as explorations of stable situations where costs and benefits are clear. Other types of theory are more suited for discussing how categories emerge from interaction.

Finally, there are important features of social life that we don't normally select in a conscious way, such as ethnic identity or religious affiliation. Social behavior is driven by our ethnicity, gender, economic background, religion, and so forth. These traits are typically ascribed rather than achieved, to use a popular distinction in sociology. Ethnicity is assigned to us long before we have the capability to question it. Social context definitely affects how we view our identity but not always in ways that are clearly described as choices. In fact, much research shows that judgments based on social traits such as race are often made much more quickly than judgments that deal with logic, such as completing a simple math problem. Thus, much of what is done in the social world is about "gut reactions," a habitus, to use one of the terms given in chapter 2, and less about choice. For example, recent research that investigates how managers in firms evaluate employees suggests that network ties between managers, which are based on shared traits, influence the evaluation. Other research shows how managers' identities, which are not strategically chosen, influence how people observe and evaluate organizations.[47]

These criticisms are not meant to persuade the reader that rational choice is without value. My view is the opposite. Rational choice seems well suited to studying many of the kinds of processes that intrigue sociologists, such as marriage or voting. People do have well-defined preferences for spouses or political candidates. Nevertheless, the criticisms of rational choice have value because they draw attention to issues of long-standing concern and encourage theoretical innovation among sociologists who focus on cost–benefit judgments in their explanations.

· · ·

This chapter has reviewed the different ways that social researchers think about the translation of goals and preferences into outcomes. Explanations that focus on decision making are appealing in some ways. They are parsimonious and emphasize things that are clearly important: resources, incentives, and competition. The main difference between economics-inspired rational-choice analysis and more sociological theories, such as social capital, is that the latter discusses group structure and behavior, whereas classical rational-choice theory focuses mainly on individual decision making. These underlying features of resource and strategy theories may also be viewed as liabilities. It is not always the case that a simple parsimonious analysis yields the best answer. Identities change, utility may be interdependent, and social structures may factor into individual preferences in important ways.

Nevertheless, it is an important theory to consider, and debates over rational choice have led to novel theoretical developments. So what are the major lessons of rational choice in sociology? What should the skeptics take away from this discussion?

First, rational-choice theory is often a good starting point for thinking about the processes that sociologists like to examine, especially when there is a clearly defined goal and a set of alternatives that can be assessed. For example, social movements are often trying to obtain some concession from a government. Would it be better to make friends with legislators or to challenge them in some way? Which allies would be good to work with—the mainstream group or the more radical group? The choices that movements face can be a matter of life or death. Protesting the Qadaffi regime in Libya could lead to imprisonment or death. Similarly, governments frequently consider the utility of their options. Should an oppressive regime liberalize and thus invite instability? Should it become more repressive and invite sanction? This insight led to one of Charles Tilly's most insightful books on protest, *From Mobilization to Revolution* (1978), which uses rational-choice theory to examine exactly when protest movements erupt and how governments respond. Rational-choice theory offers a way, at the very least, to talk about these issues in systematic ways.

Second, the debate over rational-choice theory has led to innovative ways of thinking about social structure. Social capital theory, garbage-can models, and weak-ties theory were created in the wake of the classic rational-choice model. My view is that these models are attempts to integrate ideas about social structure with theories of individual choice. Such integration would probably not have happened were there not a theory that first downplayed social structure when talking about choice. The tension between "vulgar" rational choice and the ongoing dialogue about structure and culture within classical sociology resulted in numerous attempts to find a "third way," which has been fruitful to consider.

Finally, rational-choice theory is important because it focuses relentlessly on a fundamental feature of human nature—its instrumentality. Human beings are complex, but it is undeniable that they want things and use their intelligence to get them. Some questions about instrumental action are beyond rational choice. There is no way within the theory to ask why people desire particular things. It is also difficult for rational-choice theory to discuss the "menu of options" that each society offers. But rational-choice theory is a useful way to describe any situation where there are clearly defined costs, benefits, and trade-offs. And that covers a great deal of ground.

4

VALUES AND SOCIAL STRUCTURES

AMERICAN politicians love school-reform plans, and President George W. Bush was not different. Like so many governors and presidents before him, President Bush promised that things were going to be different *this* time. With a supportive Republican legislature behind him, Bush delivered a bold law in 2001: the No Child Left Behind (NCLB) Act. According to the law, every student was instructed to take a state-wide standardized test.[1] Schools that consistently underperformed had to develop an improvement plan. If students didn't show improvement, teachers could be fired, and funds might be lost. This legislation was a new chapter in American educational history. Until the NCLB Act, standardized tests were not required for federal funding, and school evaluation was left to state and local governments.

One might think that this law would have been very popular. Max Weber, the great theorist of the rationalized society, told us that the modern capitalist society is about discipline, order, and measurement. After all, America produced Frederick Taylor, the management guru of the early twentieth century. Taylor imagined a world where business management would be no different than engineering. Managers would consult with scientists to come up with rules to tell each worker what to do. Why not apply the same logic to schooling? If standardization can make a business run better, why can't it be applied to schools? Science, not emotions, would rule the classroom.

The opposite happened. Teachers criticized NCLB in the harshest terms. Some of this reaction was predictable. Teachers hated the law because it created extra work for them. In addition to their lesson plans, they had to prepare students for standardized tests, and the policy limited their ability to manage their classes as they saw fit.[2] The public also eventually came to detest the law. For example, a Gallup poll in 2009 showed that only 21 percent of respondents felt that the law had improved schools.[3] The negative response revealed something important about schools. Teachers weren't complaining just about stress and workload but also about how NCLB changed schooling itself. By requiring students to do well on standardized tests, the law required teachers to reduce favored activities in order to "teach to the test."[4]

From one perspective, this criticism of NCLB was to be expected. Workers often resent new regulations and increased stress. But there was a deeper issue at stake in the fight over NCLB. The public and the teachers have very different views of education. Teachers see their job as a careful balancing act. Because they have close interaction with children, they believe they are in the best position to determine what children need. The freedom that many teachers have is one of the main reasons that people join that profession.[5] The public, as manifested by voters and the politicians who want to show that they care about schools, has a different view. Teachers need less discretion. They need to stick to the rules.

Thus, NCLB draws our attention to a peculiar feature of the American educational system. Our schools don't always match with our commonly held beliefs about teaching. Americans tend to believe that schools should teach the "three Rs"—reading, writing, and arithmetic—but schools are designed to do something else: allow teachers to customize classrooms in any way they see fit. Some teachers may use a traditional curriculum, whereas others may experiment, and yet others may simply not teach at all. In fact, much of the history of education reform is about how teachers resist various attempts to measure or standardize their work. Schools shield their work from intrusive outsiders and are quite pleased with the situation.[6]

The mismatch between the reformer's desires and actual school organization points to a fundamental issue in sociological theory. Our beliefs about the world, the ideas that motivate and guide our actions, aren't always aligned with our social structures. This "decoupling," as it is called in the literature on schooling, needs explanation.[7] What allows such an important institution, education, to be disconnected from the public that supports it? When is tight coupling between social values and other institutions possible?

This discussion of schools illustrates a broader theoretical issue—the link between ideas, beliefs, and structures. This chapter describes a family of theories that offer different accounts of how beliefs and attitudes (values) may or may not be aligned with patterns of roles and social behaviors (structures). These theories are varied and often conflict with each other, but they do share a strong concern with what people think, how they act, and how these actions may (or may not) lead to aggregate social outcomes. The fight over NCLB illustrates the need for such theories. If one believes that our structures and ideas are well aligned, then one needs to explain why teachers successfully resisted standardized testing and why schools made it easy for them to do so. If one believes that our institutions and our beliefs are often at odds, then one must explain what happens when they are forced together. These varied theories address one of sociology's core questions: How do societies provide structures that translate collective ideas into practice?

In the following sections, I present a scheme for understanding the different types of sociological theories that discuss the interplay of values and structures. The issue is that sociologists often disagree about the extent to which values and structures agree with each other. Thus, one can imagine a spectrum of social theory, from those sociologists who would argue for a "tight fit" between beliefs and structures to those who would argue for a weak connection. After presenting this conceptual scheme, I then discuss specific examples. Each is chosen because it illustrates a specific approach to values or structures or is an unusually good illustration of how this type of social theory leads to mechanism-based explanation. Early on, we'll encounter a classic example of theories and research that tightly connect values and structures and then explore theories that present a looser connection. Then we'll explore cultural theories that treat social structures as things that individuals interpret and actively manipulate.

LINKING VALUES AND STRUCTURES

The basic elements of a "values and structures" theory are simple. First, there are "social values," by which I simply mean the values shared among a group of people. In America, for example, we value democracy and political participation. We also value economic success and encourage people to seek financial gains. Second, there are "social structures." This term has many definitions, but in this book I use the simple and intuitive definition given in Oxford's *Dictionary of Sociology*: "A term referring to any recurring pattern of social behaviour; or, more specifically, to the ordered interrelationships between the different elements of a social system or society."[8] The term *structure* is sufficient in the present context because it captures the idea that societies have patterns of activities, such as people showing up to work, attending school, and so forth.

Values are quite different than structures. The former is psychological in nature, a description of what happens in the mind. Values reflect group psychology. The latter is defined as behavior, what people do.[9] The important question for a sociologist is how values and structures are related. Do social structures actually carry out the edicts of the collective mind? Or do people consistently behave in ways that deviate from social values?

Sociologists have answered these questions in many different ways. The answers vary along one dimension that I call *alignment*. Sociologists who believe in strong alignment tend to see values and social structures as tightly coupled or well integrated. Weak-alignment theories tend to view values as something that must be recognized but not always followed. Personal and public interests don't coincide, and there are many opportunities to deviate.

Readers familiar with the history of sociology will immediately identify numerous examples of strong-alignment theories. Perhaps the most famous is Talcott Parsons's theory of structural functionalism.[10] Even though most sociologists no longer subscribe to functionalism, there is value in talking about it because it is a very vivid example of a theory that posits a strong alignment between values and social behavior. It is also an important example because much of modern sociology, such as cultural sociology, was created when sociologists rejected functionalism and tried to answer questions about social order and culture with new ideas.

The basic argument of functionalism is that societies can be coherent and orderly if there are specific institutions that enforce solidarity. Schools teach children about good citizenship, the law punishes deviants, and so forth. The mechanisms promoting order vary. Legal institutions, for example, use the state to coerce people who deviate. Schools socialize people so that they want to conform to society's rules. Parsons also provided a historical picture. As societies develop from small tribes to modern industrial societies, they use surplus wealth to pay for people to perform certain functions that ensure the continuity of the social system: a political class of people who manage the legal system or a punitive system designed to manage deviance or professional managers who make economic decisions. Overall, though, society, according to the functionalists, is characterized by how social institutions, such as schools, express value and how these institutions result in social order.

In modern times, though, one is much less likely to find a sociologist who believes in such a strong link between values and social structures. For example, in 1977 John W. Meyer and Brian Rowan published an influential article in the *American Journal of Sociology* that provided a description of society that was starkly different from the one developed by Parsons. Parsons started with the premise that people are socialized; human beings are sponges who absorb social values. Children readily learn what they are taught, and schools explain to young people what they need to know to function in modern society. Therefore, in this view one can expect a convergence of values and structures. Because of socialization, people want what society is giving them.

Meyer and Rowan's article "Institutional Organizations: Formal Structure as Myth and Ceremony" (1977) presents a very different view of social life. This view emphasizes the decoupling of values and behavior. Meyer and Rowan do not assume that individuals are strongly socialized. They argue that people within organizations play a type of game that they call "myth and ceremony." The people who operate an organization, such as a school or a corporation, must ensure that they have resources to do so. The school principal needs tax money, just as the CEO needs investor funds. To acquire these resources, organizations establish their legitimacy by adopting policies and operating procedures that meet with public approval—even if the public statements about policies and procedures have little to do with what actually happens inside the organization. Thus, values become "myths," and structures become "ceremonies" designed to make the public happy. These ceremonies eventually take a life of their own and become routine parts of organizations.

Meyer and Rowan's work was inspired by their research on schools. In a series of papers in the 1970s, Meyer, Rowan, and their collaborators found that school policies did not always accurately describe what actually happened inside schools.[11] If teachers are so disconnected from the administration, then what is the point of administrative documents? Why do school boards spend so much time detailing the curriculum or developing a discipline policy if teachers in their isolated classrooms can ignore it? The answer, according to Meyer and Rowan's "myth-and-ceremony" hypothesis, is that these policies show legitimacy and adherence to social values. To be accredited, schools must show the public that they teach proper subjects, and parents want to know that students are disciplined in appropriate ways. To flaunt these values is to invite the public's rejection and the closing of the school. However, the policies do not automatically mean that people are enforcing the rules. Rather, they are a gloss on the organization that allows everyone inside to go about business as usual.

I discuss functionalism and myth-and-ceremony theory because they represent the range of theoretical possibilities. Functionalism is rightly considered a fairly rigid theory of social order, which is one of the reasons why sociologists no longer countenance it. Myth-and-ceremony theory represents the opposite extreme: organizations can easily insulate themselves from the public, and the result is a social system of loosely connected pieces. The subsequent sections discuss how modern sociology grapples with the issue of how values and social structures come together.

CONTEMPORARY SOCIAL SYSTEMS THEORY

Modern sociology contains many traditions that focus on how values and structures come together. One tradition, which I call "social systems theory," likes to see society as some sort of organic entity. It is a theory of strong alignment and sees itself as a natural successor to earlier theories of strong alignment, such as functionalism. Not surprisingly, these sociologists are often inspired by functionalism but try to address functionalism's limitations. In the 1980s, for example, Jeffrey Alexander promoted "neofunctionalism," which retains the main ideas of structural functionalism, such as social integration, but openly discusses conflict and interaction.[12] Later, Alexander developed a specific argument about social solidarity that relies on performance and rituals, which he called "cultural pragmatics."[13] The main argument of cultural pragmatics is that performances, such as religious rituals, poetry, and film, can promote social solidarity by evoking intense emotions that encourage people to coordinate their actions with others. Social performances depend on a stock of ideas, scripts, texts, and characters that might be familiar to performer and audience. The performer creates a specific utterance from this set of ideas and thus translates abstract scripts into concrete actions for an audience to view. Successful performance depends on how well the performer can make the audience identify with the performer and link their experience to what they already know from other performances. In smaller, preindustrial societies, the performer interacted with the entire social group, whereas in modern societies there are specialists—actors, speech makers, and so forth—who speak to a larger mass audience and appeal to their common experience. Thus, performances have not only content but also social functions in connecting the performer and audience to some broader ideas. Rituals persist because they allow people to develop a sense of community. The ultimate purpose of Alexander's theory is to explain how modern societies still might "hang together" even though there is no longer any opportunity for everyone to bond with each other through face-to-face rituals, such as tribal dance. Solidarity emerges when some performer uses mass media to convey a story to coordinate behavior. The mechanism between values and actual solidarity is the performance and the emotional feelings triggered by the performance.

Alexander applies this theory, that cultural performances link disparate audiences in modern society, to a wide range of phenomena, such as theater and political speech. One particularly interesting example is terrorism.[14] As many observers have noted, terrorism is quite unlike other forms of political violence. Its immediate goal is simply to maim, murder, and humiliate civilians rather than to destroy an opposing military force. Terrorism is a symbolic and a physical act aimed at humiliation, not conquest. Furthermore, terrorists often want the target state to repress its citizens and thus to validate the terrorists' criticism of that state.

In Alexander's view, terrorism is a performance that triggers additional counterperformances. It is a violent humiliation of the target that is intended to provoke repressive actions that will further justify the terrorists' cause. However, terrorism may have unintended effects. As Alexander and others have noted about the attacks on September 11, 2001, the World Trade Center became a powerful symbol that rallied Americans. It is true that the American state changed and become more punitive, but it is also true that terrorism created sympathy between American citizens and the state. The attacks strengthened the political position of American leaders. This newfound political strength then allowed for another performance, the invasion of Afghanistan and Iraq, which was meant as a symbol that the United States took terrorism seriously. The American public and the world would clearly see that such violence would not go unpunished.

The other well-known social systems theorist was Niklas Luhmann, who viewed structures and values as two faces of the same process. Once people focus on their group identity, that identity provides directions for how different social elements (people, groups, organizations) are to be created, linked, and manipulated. The emergent social structure will then allow people to learn what they need to know to re-create the structure or modify it. Luhmann's account of social structure is analogous to how cells contain instructions for their creation and future reproduction. Borrowing from biology, Luhmann claimed that social systems are "autopoeitic," which means that the social system generates itself; it is recursive.[15] For example, Luhmann argued that mass media has this property. Journalists respond to stories written by other journalists. The meaning of the media is defined by other media in a circular fashion.[16] From this (very brief) summary of Luhmann's ideas, we can see another type of mechanism employed by systems theorists. Values and social order are strongly correlated because of learning and signaling. People are embedded in specific social systems in which they learn the rules. Through learning, they copy the social system. The journalist learns the rules of journalism from other journalists, and journalists run their newspapers and websites the way they were run before, creating another generation of sociotechnical systems.

INSTITUTIONS, INSTITUTIONS, INSTITUTIONS

Social systems theory is only one way to describe the link between social values and social structures, and in general it tends to argue for strong alignment between values and structures. What is much more common in sociology is a style of theory known as "institutionalism," wherein scholars offer mechanisms that discuss how social environments may or may not regulate the behavior of individuals and organizations. Institutionalism in its different manifestations views values and structures as being less strongly aligned, which is why some versions of institutionalism often speak of "decoupling." Meyer and Rowan's myth-and-ceremony argument is frequently cited as an example of a loose-coupling theory.

To understand this turn in modern social theory, it helps to discuss the term *institution* and why sociologists care so much about the concept. A common definition is that an institution is a rule that governs a specific kind of behavior.[17] For example, standardized testing in education might be considered such a rule. Most colleges require applicants to submit scores from the SAT or other standardized tests. The law does not require standardized testing, but most colleges do it anyway. In fact, standardized testing is so common in higher education that it has attracted considerable criticism as an inflexible and unfair way to evaluate students.

Institutional theories in general try to explain how institutions are created, modified, or eliminated. A typical institutional theory tries to explain the relationship between these rules and observed patterns of behavior. Another typical feature of institutional theories is that they try to explain how these rules of behavior may or may not be accurate reflections of social values. Thus, all institutional theories are attempts to explain the link between values and structures. They are the rules or standards that provide specific instructions on how individuals should act in ways that will make them appear legitimate in the eyes of the public.

It is illuminating to compare a traditional functionalist analysis of standardized testing with an institutional analysis. A classical functionalist approach might argue that standardized tests are required in an advanced society that needs a highly trained workforce. As the division of labor grows, there is a shift to knowledge-based labor, which requires that students be sorted according to academic ability. Thus, there arises a need for an institution (standardized testing) to identify and reward the people who would benefit most from higher education.[18]

In contrast, institutional scholars might frame standardized testing as an expression of social values—"rationalized myths" that people try to translate into concrete social practices. Scholars ask if it is really the case that standardized tests exist primarily as an efficient tool for sorting students according to academic ability. For example, many colleges are known to use criteria other than standardized testing in selecting students. Students may be granted admission because they belong to an underrepresented ethnic group, are athletes, or are children of donors and alumni. Other critics point out that standardized tests scores have limited predictive power. Test scores give a rough estimate of an applicant's academic ability and are of limited use in evaluating applicants within a narrow range of scores (e.g., applicants to highly competitive schools who have similar grades and scores). In other words, colleges routinely minimize standardized test scores for students who fulfill the colleges' political or financial needs, and it is common knowledge that standardized tests are less than perfect predictors of future performance.[19]

An institutionalist might then argue that colleges use test scores for more than just sorting students according to ability.

Standardized tests can be used for legitimizing admission office choices and facilitating a wide range of potentially illegitimate actions. One might argue that standardized test scores are an example of "myth and ceremony," as described by Meyer and Rowan. Thus, the use of required standardized tests seems to indicate that a college is choosing students according to rational and impersonal rules but at the same time provides "cover" for relaxing those standards. Colleges might actually be selecting students in part on the basis of personal connections or athletic ability.[20] The loose connection between norms and actual behavior is one way that a modern understanding of institutions leads to a theory of weak alignment.

Theories of myth and decoupling aren't the only versions of institutionalism. In 1983, Paul DiMaggio and Walter Powell published a highly influential article, "The Iron Cage Revisited: Institutional Isomorphism and Collective Rationality in Organizational Fields," claiming that organizations were subject to strong external pressures. In their view, organizational leaders operate in a world of uncertainty where it is not easy or feasible to know exactly what to do. This uncertainty means that organizations, such as colleges or firms, may copy each other, do what is promoted by professional elites, and do what is required by law or custom. Institutional imperatives induce uniformity among people and organizations, and these taken-for-granted rules govern behavior within each given sector, such as education. Social pressures create an "iron cage" of rules and expectations that must be obeyed. Organizations and their policies can operate only when they obey these social expectations. In DiMaggio and Powell's account, there is no distinctive behavior within organizations. Everything is done to conform to social expectations.

Their argument became very popular in sociology and related fields because it addressed the social aspects of administrative behavior. When discussing firms, for example, scholars commonly explain internal structure as a matter of efficiency. In one famous example, business historian Alfred Chandler claimed in the early 1960s that the multidivisional firm (the "M-form") was created to solve information problems within massive organizations, such as Sears and DuPont.[21] Complex manufacturing and marketing processes require that the firm develop a vertical structure where specialized divisions report to a central office, who then prepares concise reports for executives. Later, organizational sociologists, such as Neil Fligstein, argued that this was not the case. The adoption of M-form was not always linked to firm size or to other features that indicate complexity. It was instead linked to the arrival of professionalized managers who promoted the new management fad, the M-form.[22] The institutionalist "move" in Fligstein's analysis is the shift from efficiency to developments in the world of professional managers as an explanation for the M-form.

What is important about the DiMaggio and Powell argument is that it represents a very popular example of a strong-alignment theory within the broader tradition of institutional theory. It is particularly popular among sociologists because it explains social order and conformity to social norms without recourse to functionality or efficiency. Unlike the theory promoted by Parsons or by his successors, such as Alexander and Luhmann, the new versions of institutionalism require only that people want their organization to succeed and appear legitimate. They do not require that people maximize profits, nor do they require an argument that social institutions accomplish some goal for the community. In terms of empirical research, DiMaggio and Powell's institutionalism is easy to implement because a researcher can track the spread of a practice, such as accountability in schools, and ascribe the spread to the desire to appear legitimate.

It is also important to compare DiMaggio and Powell's institutionalism with Meyer and Rowan's myth-and-ceremony theory. Both are institutional theories, but they yield different conclusions. DiMaggio and Powell's more rigid theory argues that people are highly susceptible to social pressures. They may have weak commitments or no commitments and are willing to do what appears to be socially acceptable. In contrast, myth-and-ceremony theory assumes that people retain their commitments in the face of social pressure and find ways to evade social pressure and pursue their own interests.

It is also instructive to consider the mechanisms offered by these two theories. Meyer and Rowan's myth-and-ceremony theory explains the weak link between values and structures by recourse to monitoring costs and a lack of organizational transparency. The executive realizes that it is impossible for the shareholders to closely monitor all that goes in the firm. Thus, the organization itself acts as a shield. It is simply too difficult and expensive to watch all employees. DiMaggio and Powell's "iron cage" theory argues that when fields, or populations of organizations (e.g., schools), are well established and have clear rules for conduct, people essentially monitor themselves. They watch the environment for clues about how to behave (e.g., what high-status schools do is a signal for lower-status schools) and then implement these practices. In other cases, institutionalists argue that external forces, such as the state or professional groups, will monitor and enforce the rules. Hospitals will be run by doctors, for example, who share similar views learned in medical school or from peers or will be closely monitored by the state. What these explanations share is the belief that outsiders can control organizations relatively easily. The mechanism that connects values to structures are the many different ways that outsiders are able to topple, circumvent, or overcome the barriers to monitoring.

CULTURE IN SOCIOLOGY

Cultural sociology represents a third way to think about the link between values and structures. The functionalist (and neofunctionalist) view is that institutions and social practices encourage a match between individual actions and social goals. The institutionalist view, broadly speaking, is that institutions are responses to values, but they may or may not accomplish the goal of regulating behavior. The third alternative is to assume a more interpretive view of human action. Rather than assume that human beings respond to institutions or social norms, we might argue that human beings treat social expectations in a highly instrumental manner and actively change norms or assign new meanings to them. Faced with a social norm that says, "You must do X," they might accept it, reject it, use it in some novel manner, reinterpret it, or replace it with some new norm. The distinctive feature of cultural sociology is that it acknowledges that actors are not passive receptacles for social norms, nor are they reactive. They are instead creative actors who interpret things, create things, categorize things, and argue with things. The way they do this is with the mental tools and frameworks that they have inherited from the wider culture. Thus, culture doesn't force people to do things; culture is a flexible resource that is used by people, that guides people, and can be altered by people. Thus, in explaining how people gets from X to Y, cultural sociologists offer arguments about how people create, alter, interpret, or apply the framework of ideas that their society presents to them.

Perhaps the most prominent example of modern cultural sociology is Ann Swidler's "culture as tool kit" theory.[23] Swidler starts with a direct attack on the idea of values as presented by Parsons and his followers. She, like other functionalist critics, attacks Parsons for presenting values as ahistorical things that determine what people want. In fact, Swidler argues, ideas and social practices are attached pragmatically to historical circumstance. She illustrates her argument with an interpretation of Max Weber's classic book *The Protestant Ethic and the Spirit of Capitalism* ([1905] 1958), which linked a particular worldview to an economic system. If it were the case that a belief in salvation caused an ascetic ethos, then why did that ethos of frugality persist when society became less religious? Swidler's argument is that our ideas about the world are not fashioned after decontextualized ideologies but are organized around specific social practices. The activities associated with Calvinism became associated with other secular activities, such as pursuing profits and saving money, even as people dropped the religious motivation.

In addition to arguing that tool kits for action are attached to specific practices, Swidler argues against the view that social action is necessarily rational and calculating. The situations that people encounter are often complex, and it is hard for individuals to devise optimal strategies in every situation. Social situations are informationally rich contexts where individuals must economize their cognitive efforts: "But people do not, indeed cannot, build up a sequence of actions piece by piece, striving with each act to maximize a given outcome. Action is necessarily integrated into larger assemblages, called here 'strategies of action.'"[24] Deriving the optimal response to a given situation is difficult, and thus it is better to rely on preexisting routines to cope with whatever situations arise. With this argument, Swidler deftly moves from the world of the rule follower to the world of the culture user.

Culture as a tool and guide informs *Habits of the Heart: Individualism and Commitment in American Life* (1985), a widely read book that discusses individuality and community in America. Written by Robert Bellah, Richard Madsen, William M. Sullivan, Ann Swidler, and Stephen M. Tipton, *Habits of the Heart* explains how Americans view the private and public good as well as individuality and how religion informs those sentiments. The book is a highly nuanced study of how Americans define what is valuable, especially with respect to private life, work, and community. Upon publication, it was immediately hailed as an important study of American character. It is filled with vivid interviews with Americans struggling with their lives. What is more important for the present study is the kind of argument it presents. Rather than portraying Americans as beholden to an abstract notion of "individualism," it shows people who are torn between multiple demands and who use values to help them reason about their lives, often in conflicting ways.

In one informative chapter, the authors discuss how cultural practices help Americans resolve their ambiguous relationship with the cultural ideal of individualism, which asks that people pursue financial and economic goals, often at the expense of family or communal life. Working long hours to maximize income leads to fewer hours spent with family and friends, which can decrease an individual's identification with a particular community. Religion provides one resolution for this problem because a religiously defined community provides stability that is not attainable in an individualistic framework. Another example is the use of ethnic communities. In one interview, the son of immigrants talks about how he became involved in the Boston area Italian community. Early in life, he had tried to shed his ethnic identity and assimilate, which meant de-emphasizing his Italian heritage. He followed the individualistic ethos by minimizing his group identity. He later reluctantly decided to help the Sons of Italy establish a chapter but encountered resistance because some Boston residents felt that Italians were drunken and disruptive. This experience encouraged the man to rely on his ethnic community and to accept his heritage in part because it helped him understand the problems he had in "Americanizing" early in his life.[25] The various interviews in *Habits* share this structure. People don't just accept social values. Instead, values help people resolve difficult situations and create new practices.

Sociologists such as Swidler, Wendy Griswold, and Hans Joas set the agenda within cultural sociology by relentlessly focusing on how people interpret the world, and they have recently taken such arguments in new directions. Griswold, for example, argues that our lives include "cultural objects," to which we attach meaning and symbolism.[26] Thus, an important task for cultural sociology is to understand which meanings we attach to material goods and how they fit into our wider cultural world. Joas focuses less on the material dimensions of social life and more on the cognitive aspects. For him, what is interesting about human action is its inherent improvisatory character. Human beings have an amazing capacity to create new meanings in response to unexpected situations.[27]

Swidler herself has tried to refine and extend the theory of cultural tool kits. *Talk of Love: How Culture Matters* (2001) explores ideas of love to make sense of marriages and other relationships and offers a development of her previously established major ideas. Swidler thinks that it is limiting to think of culture as being only a tool kit. Rather, culture is a set of ideas that leads to specific combinations of emotions, beliefs, and modes of action. A phrase that summarizes this view is "cultured capacities," suggesting that how we act in the social world is shaped by communal beliefs. Swidler suggests that she promotes an "identity" model of culture, which focuses on how people act in accordance to how they see themselves. The range of what actions people think are possible and appropriate are drawn from culture. This is not to say that people consistently apply ideology, but they are able to manipulate their philosophies to make sense of their world for themselves and their audiences.[28]

MECHANISMS

The previous sections presented different ways that sociologists have tried to connect values, social structures, and culture. The social systems theorists offer a variety of explanations to depict how entire societies maintain order, and institutionalists are more varied in how tightly connected values and structures are in their theories. Cultural sociologists take a different tact by explaining how moral beliefs and individual psychology interact to create strategies and retrospective accounts of action.

It is valuable to think about how sociologists in these varied traditions articulate mechanisms in their research. That is, how does one extract the underlying "recipe book" that sociologists use to explain social behavior? Socialization appears in many explanations of values and structures. For example, a common argument made by functionalists in the 1950s and 1960s was that schools, religions, and governments teach people how to behave properly. In fact, Parsons once claimed that the purpose of elementary school was to detach children from their families and reorient them toward the wider society.[29] Socialization also appears as a mechanism in more modern institutionalist accounts. For example, DiMaggio and Powell's article "The Iron Cage Revisited" (1983) suggests that organizations will conform to social expectations because the professionals who manage them share an ideology. The argument is that managers belong to occupational groups that have strong internal cultures; doctors are trained in medical schools with strict programs; accountants have well-known rules for managing funds; and so forth. The socialization that occurs within each occupation is then transmitted to the organization. Firms use similar accounting rules because accountants in general are well socialized into their profession's culture.

Some institutionalists, though, adopt a much more active type of social psychology, implying a different mechanism. Those inspired by Meyer and Rowan's article "Institutionalized Organizations" (1977) present a world where people are openly skeptical of institutions. People may acquiesce to a rule but internally reject the rule's goals, such as the teacher who claims to use the school board's official curriculum but inserts her own material. Similarly, many cultural theorists, who follow in Swidler's footsteps, ascribe a great deal of agency to individuals. People are pragmatic problem solvers who rotate through socialized routines until they find something that works. Thus, in explaining the link between culture or values and social structure, socialization is incomplete, and, as noted earlier, monitoring people is a demanding task.

The most recent work in institutional theory tries to catalog these varied behaviors that are aimed at defining or responding to social norms. In a recent article, Roy Suddaby and Tom Lawrence articulate the idea of "institutional work," by which they mean the many things people do when they encounter institutions.[30] The list is long and detailed, running from challenging institutions to replacing them to making a "vestment" or exerting the effort needed to have a stake or personal interest in some particular institution. Other scholars talk about institutional logics, which are broad patterns of beliefs and behaviors that people use to make and understand their world.[31] Accountability in education is an example. People use a general logic of monitoring, measuring, and rewarding to design schools and standardized tests.

Then we have theories that have a distinctly pragmatic and improvisatory character. Sociologists such as Ann Swidler tell us that people have the ability to improvise solutions to problems and to experiment with practices to come up with new ways of organizing and regulating social life. Hans Joas argues that all action, in some sense, is creative in that contextual factors must come into play as individuals navigate their world.[32] Drawing on George Herbert Mead's theory, Joas points out that human action goes beyond the simple chain of "thought and action." Human actions emerge in many ways, from bodily responses to social situations to active choices. This extremely brief sketch omits much of the richness of Joas's theory, but one can clearly see how modern cultural sociology traces the line from culture to action. People are embedded in specific situations that require active thinking, and they use their moral and ethical beliefs to guide their actions and to explain themselves to others, thus creating a future pattern of behavior.

THE MICRO-TO-MACRO JUMP

The analysis of values, institutions, and culture raises an important point that merits more attention: How does one construct theories that move from a description of individuals to a description of larger social groups? As we have seen so far, the debate over the relationship between structure and individual action can move from an analysis of individual emotions, as in Swidler's book *Talk of Love*, to analyses of entire societies, as in Alexander's cultural pragmatics. In sociology, this movement is called the "micro–macro" transition problem. That is, how do our theories of individual action allow us to describe larger patterns of behavior? This section discusses various answers to this question. In some cases, the explanation of the micro–macro transition is rather obvious. Structural functionalism usually relies on the theory that people are relatively easy to socialize, so the macro–micro link for this theory is fairly easy to present, and the mechanism is obvious. Once educational and legal institutions are established, they create people who know how to apply the rules and thus reproduce them over time. Good government makes good citizens, who know how to make good government.

Institutionalists are also quite concerned about making sure that their theory of individual behavior is logically consistent with their description of large-scale social processes. As noted earlier, institutionalists vary a great deal in what they predict about the connection between ideas and observed behavior. They also vary in their approaches to large-scale structure. Institutionalism of the sort promoted by DiMaggio and Powell posits a world of relative uniformity. As long as there are high-status actors who can validate norms or behavioral scripts, those norms are likely to be widely adopted and become the legitimate way of organizing society. In the 1990s, institutional theorists added extra nuance to the theory by discussing "institutional entrepreneurs" who are responsible for introducing rules and "policing" them.[33]

Myth-and-ceremony theory offers an even more nuanced approach: societies appear to be uniform at a large scale (e.g., looking at the average school), but there is great variation when one uses a microscope to examine them. What happens theoretically is that individuals evaluate rules and decide which might be in their interest to follow, endorse, or evade. Thus, there isn't a single pattern of behavior that needs to be explained. Rather, there are both a large-scale pattern that represents what the public wants organizations to accomplish and a parallel pattern of "real" behavior. This larger scale suggests to recent institutional scholars that there is an important process of enactment of norms that needs to be properly explicated. Institutions are only as real as the people who enforce or ignore them. To understand the acceptance or rejection of rules, one requires a psychological account of how these rules trigger emotional responses from the people they affect. These varying responses create both the "legitimate" social order that rules are meant to create and a shadow order.

Modern action theorists, such as Swidler and Joas, for the most part don't concern themselves with explanations of large-scale social structure. They do note that culture emerges from specific practices that are attached to particular environments that are defined by repeated situations. There is no "ideology of love and marriage." Rather, people create an ideology of love as they participate in their marriages, which are repeated interactions between two people in the context of creating a home, raising children, and so forth. Thus, the thrust of cultural sociology, pragmatism, and related theories is to identify the often tacit emotional or subconscious basis of action and then link that basis to specific contexts.

Just because cultural theorists don't focus on explaining the emergence of aggregate social structure, one isn't forbidden from trying to extrapolate or suggest how such theories might make the link from small-group or individual psychology to larger structures. One might take the ideas of cultural sociology and append them or merge them with institutional theories. For example, Swidlerian cultural sociology might be a microsociological foundation for the types of "institutional work" that people engage in. Individuals, in such a theory, would be described via tool kits instead of preferences, and institutions are the large-scale patterns that emerge from such a theory. Another approach would be for cultural sociologists and action theorists to define some alternative to macrosociological concepts such as "institution." Cultural theorists and others already have their own distinctive ideas (see chapter 5), such as "frame" or "interaction order," that describe the situations that people jointly create, but much work remains in teasing out a distinctive macrotheory implied by such concepts.

Then, of course, one could argue that this distinction between individual action and larger social structure is bogus. The microlevel and macrolevel processes are so intertwined, so dependent on each other, that it is misleading to draw a line between them. Even offering a mechanism-based account creates a distinction that does not need to be made. This argument, called "structuration" theory, was offered by Anthony Giddens as an alternative to traditional arguments about whether social action is best understood as the result of individual volition, rational or otherwise, or is guided primarily by larger social forces.[34] The central idea of Giddens's structuration theory is that actions and structures are recursive. Action defines and modifies structure and structure defines action. The newly modified structure then provides options, constraints, and other limits on action.

· · ·

This chapter has described a vast realm of sociology inspired by two simple observations: one is that people tend to have shared beliefs about what is good, and the other is that people create social structures, such as the state and the family. The question that naturally arises is how these two observations are connected. The arguments covered represent the various ways sociologists have tried connecting culture and structure, and they reflect the complexity of the problem. Describing how worldviews or moral systems influence action is challenging itself, and then making the jump to large-scale structure is even more challenging. Nevertheless, this rich set of ideas can be usefully mapped out by asking how each sociologist moves from X to Y.

5

SOCIAL CONSTRUCTION

OCIOLOGISTS will often say, "*This* is socially constructed."
And *this* might be something that is not usually thought
of as "social" at all, such as science or medicine. It is not
surprising, then, that social construction often strikes people
as odd. How can it possibly be the case that apparently objective things such as science are influenced by social beliefs? This
chapter starts with an illustration of what sociologists mean by
"social construction" and why things such as science are usefully
described as social constructions. Then it offers a basic outline
of what social construction means in general and focuses on a
few dimensions of social construction. After that, it reviews more
recent arguments about how social construction happens in various sociological studies.

To help you appreciate what the term *social construction* means,
I appeal to an argument made by the philosopher John Searle in
his book *The Construction of Social Reality* (1997). Some things
are true independently of what we think of them, and others
are only true because of what we think of them. He called these
two types of facts "institutional" and "brute" facts. For example,
"Mount Everest is taller than any other mountain," and "Barack
Obama is the president of the United States" are true statements,

but they are fundamentally different kinds of statements. The first statement refers to a physical fact that exists independently of what anyone believes. No matter what I think, the pile of stone known as "Mount Everest" reaches a greater height than any other pile of stone on earth. In contrast, the president of the United States is a social construction. The human being known as Barack Obama is considered president only because of an election. That election is considered valid only because it follows the rules set out in the U.S. Constitution and various state laws. Those laws are considered valid only because they were approved by various legislatures. The laws themselves rest on a foundation of belief and opinion, not on physical reality. If everyone were to decide that Obama is no longer president, then he would no longer be president in any real sense. Yet we consider the presidency to be a real thing and the power wielded by political executives to be equally real.

Searle's argument makes an important distinction about the nature of the world. There are physical facts, such as the relative location of planets, and there are social or institutional facts, such as the meaning of laws. What sociology adds to this basic observation is that social construction occurs whenever people come together. For example, when scientists look at stars, they must create a shared social understanding of what they are looking at. The scientist who looks at stars in 2016 comes equipped with Albert Einstein's theory of relativity. Her counterpart in the 1800s would have a different set of ideas to guide his science. He would have only the classical celestial mechanics of Isaac Newton and Johannes Kepler. In both cases, the physical reality would be the same, but what the community of science believes and acts upon would differ. Further, these differences would not merely be responses to observation; they would also reflect social and cultural attitudes within science and the world at large.

This chapter breaks down social construction theory as it appears in sociology into a handful of social processes or mechanisms that shape how people jointly create their social world. It describes these building blocks of social construction theory— rituals, framing, and knowledge stocks—in detail and offers canonical accounts of each process. It then explores how social construction theory has been applied to various topics. I discuss Thomas Kuhn's classic account of scientific development from a social construction perspective and use recent sociological research on stock markets to investigate how social constructions can shape "real" things such as the American economy, touching on newer developments in social constructionism, such as performativity theory. Thus, the chapter moves from an overview of how social construction operates in sociology to a discussion of social construction's consequences.

SOCIAL CONSTRUCTION = FRAMING + COPRESENCE + KNOWLEDGE

The description of social construction that I present here relies on three ideas that have gained prominence in sociology: ritual chains, framing, and the stock of knowledge. The term *ritual chain* refers to a sequence of meetings of people where they gather, interact, and further define their reality. For example, in a firm executives show up to weekly strategy meetings, argue about the state of the market, and develop a view of where the economy is going and how their firm fits into the picture. These executive meetings are then linked with other meetings that include midlevel managers, engineers, and other staff. Framing is a concept introduced by Erving Goffman that draws attention to how people assign meaning to their situation.[1] In the example of executive strategy meetings, the executive may decide that this week's meeting will be routine or that the meeting should be used to challenge the firm's leadership. Finally, social construction usually entails the creation of knowledge, which then becomes part of the background of interactions. Returning to the example of our fictional firm, it might be the case that the chief financial officer was fired at a meeting because he invested too much of the firm's funds into financial derivatives. Thus, part of the firm's history now includes the firing of this executive. and now everyone knows that financial derivatives are too risky. In other words, these routine meetings leave behind "facts" that become part of the firm's informal knowledge that people learn as they work there.

This approach provides a way to unpack social construction so as to reveal the mechanisms leading from cause to effect. The logical requirement for social construction is for people to meet. Without copresence, there would be no communication, no sharing of values, and no conflict. The final effect is that people come to believe something, and it is real for them. That final outcome is the stock of knowledge. The in-between part, the mechanism, is how people assign meaning to the facts that they are trying to understand—the framing. The next section explores each of these three ideas in detail and then different examples of social construction are offered.

CHAINS, FRAMES, AND FACTS

Randall Collins formulates the theory of interaction ritual chains in a book titled *Interaction Ritual Chains* (2004), starting with some simple observations. First, groups precede social construction. That is, there must be some group that will come together to develop shared beliefs. The group must meet with some frequency and have social practices that encourage group membership. In other words, the starting point is the situation—moments where people come together in shared awareness. The sociology of science provides excellent examples. Scientists come together on a daily basis in their laboratories. The process of setting up experiments, writing grant proposals, and performing analysis brings scientists together frequently. Academia is another example of where scientists come together. They gather daily in lecture halls and seminar rooms. They pass judgments on dissertations and journal article submissions.

Second, Collins focuses on emotional resonance. It is not enough that people gather; they must also have a strong emotional attachment to the situation, which leads them to invest in the group and its ideas. For example, scientists often seek rewards for the science they produce. Perhaps they want a higher salary from the university. They may have a personal interest in a particular theory due to its aesthetic features (e.g., the theory is "elegant"), or the theory is promoted by scholars that they like. They might also desire recognition or praise from their fellow scientists. The result is that scientists invest emotional energy in the routines of science and the academy. The dissertation defense isn't a dispassionate discussion of student research. It is something that triggers senior scholars' impassioned attention, ensuring that the ritual will be performed again in the future.

Gathering people and creating emotional resonance are two processes that have always drawn attention from scholars interested in interaction and social construction. Collins adds a few more theoretical arguments that expand his theory. One is the insistence on group barriers, which sociologists often call "boundary making." An essential part of social construction is *social*. Certainly copresence, or the physical gathering of people, is an aspect of this sociality. But barriers are also equally important. The *who* is just as important as the *how*. The scientist, for example, requires that other people possess a minimal amount of knowledge about his or her subject. Conversations about teaching and research are not conducted by a random collection of people. Rather, to participate in the scientific conversation often means subjecting oneself to years of scientific training. Even among themselves, scientists will make judgments about who is allowed to voice an opinion on specific topics.

In contrast, other group interaction depends on extremely porous barriers. For example, the legitimacy of democratic politics often depends on the ability of the "average person" to speak or participate. Voting is one common form of political participation, but there are many others. Consider the American school board meeting. It is common practice for schools to be governed by a panel of elected officials. School boards have meetings where anyone may walk up to the microphone and speak directly to the school board members. Even when political gatherings are tightly controlled and scripted, political figures in democracies will try to establish the appearance of openness. Presidential debates are a classic example. In modern times, debates between presidential candidates are often presented in a "town hall" format where people in the audience—average middle-class Americans—ask candidates questions. Although the questions no doubt reflect genuine concerns about the economy, they are nonetheless scripted and controlled by the staff. When "average Americans" openly argue with political candidates, they become news items. For example, businessman and conservative activist Herman Cain received his first dose of national media attention by arguing with Bill Clinton in a "town hall" meeting in 1994. In contrast, school board members are used to periodic arguments with aggrieved parents and teachers. Although not a daily occurrence, argument is such a routine feature of the school board meeting that it is completely unremarkable.

Collins makes the leap to large-scale social process with the idea of the "ritual chain," which means a series of interrelated group meetings and their associated rituals. Churches have weekly services. Scientists have annual conferences. These are highly formal examples, but the social world is filled with other, more informal ritual chains. Collins draws our attention to sex. People create environments where it is entirely normal to seek out sex in routine ways. Consider the college "hookup" scene that has drawn so much recent attention. Prior to the 1960s, college students were supposed to have sex only within the confines of marriage. Since then, colleges have liberalized, and there has emerged a system of dormitories, Greek organizations, and private spaces where people gather to drink and seek out casual sexual partners. The pattern is simple—one arrives at a social gathering, drinks alcohol, and then flirts with potential partners. Norms emerge that govern what is acceptable and what different signals mean. The hookup scene is a great example of a ritual chain because its constituent components are easy to identify. The party is the gathering. People have a clear emotional investment. Barriers are set up so that only specific people may show up. Most important, for Collins, is the fact that the chain is rather obvious. Once people internalize the rules of the hookup scene, the scene is fairly easy to re-create with other partners. Indeed, all one needs for a good party is a building, some alcoholic beverages, and contacts with people who already know the rules of the game. Thus, it should not be surprising that the hookup scene has become a widespread feature of college social life in the 2000s. Note that this example is used to illustrate the underlying logic of Collins's argument, not to endorse the hookup scene, which has attracted much criticism because it institutionalizes male-dominant sexual encounters and exposes women to assault.[2]

Erving Goffman's theory of interaction and ritual provides an extra analysis of social construction that explains how one moves from groups to social construction. Goffman uses the metaphor of the theater stage to describe how people create their reality.[3] Human interactions are a series of performances based on shared understandings of what an interaction is about. In Goffman's book *The Presentation of the Self in Everyday Life* (1959), every person has a private and public self, a demeanor that is shown to others. The public self is designed to manage expectations and emotions that protect the private self. A person may refuse to speak up in a business meeting to avoid embarrassment but may internally have very strong opinions. A homosexual woman may publically display heterosexual behaviors but have unrevealed preferences for women. Goffman tended to see all interactions in these terms. The meeting of two people is a potentially dangerous situation that is defused through impression management. All of us have private selves who wish to preserve our "face" through elaborate games and rituals. The failure of any of these games leads to conflict and embarrassment. The public face is flimsy, and the "backstage" is revealed. Then we have strong feelings of embarrassment that remind us to do a better job of playing the game.

Goffman linked the presentation of the self to group context with the concept of the interaction ritual. Once an individual offers a presentation of self, a face, it is often expected that others accept the framing of the situation and "carry the line."[4] Thus, many interactions acquire a ritualistic character with individuals trying to maintain their "face." Individuals' personal front sets the term of the interaction through their gesture, demeanor, dress, and speech, and others are expected to reciprocate. Thus, social life is not just about people presenting themselves; it's about how often others accept this presentation and then repeat the interaction.

Goffman also explained social reality in terms of group process. One particularly valuable concept is the "frame," the meaning attached to a particular situation. The theory of social frames is that for any performance to have meaning, the audience has to agree on what that meaning might be.[5] For example, politicians are constantly working on framing political issues. In the debate over health-care reform in 2010, congressional Democrats and the White House depicted the issue as one of health-care access. Republicans offered the opposing frame that health-care reforms should be about market liberalization instead of about increasing government spending and budget deficits. Each political faction sought to influence voters, who would judge the legislation based on how it was framed. These frames served their political purpose. Polls indicated that many voters thought that health care was an unjustified expansion of government power, but the same polls often showed that they approved of individual measures designed to increase access to health care.

Peter Berger and Thomas Luckmann's approach to social construction focuses on how these routine meetings and framings aggregate to a larger social reality. In their book *The Social Construction of Reality* (1966), Berger and Luckmann point out that an individual's perception of the world is based on a stock of facts that are learned and reinforced through social interaction. One's "common sense" is not obvious; it emerges from repeated interactions with family, friends, and coworkers. These commonly held beliefs then allow for the creation and elaboration of an "objective" social reality. Once ideas become habitual, they become, as Berger and Luckmann put it, "institutionalized." Ideas acquire a taken-for-granted quality and appear to be durable aspects of the social world. This socially constructed reality is held together by signs that allow for coordination and consensus and by enforcers who punish those who deviate from prescribed behaviors. Berger and Luckmann's account focuses on communal processes and is essentially phenomenological. That is, their theory of social reality depends on a community's "social facts" and how these facts are used to build the reality that people inhabit. But instead of assuming a "material basis" for social life, as a Marxist might, social order is constructed entirely through individual experiences that are shaped by Goffman's framings and Collins's ritualized interactions.

KUHN AND SOCIAL CONSTRUCTION

One of the most famous modern examples of a social construction argument comes from Thomas Kuhn's book *The Structure of Scientific Revolutions* (1962). Although Kuhn is usually remembered as a philosopher of science, his work is a sociological analysis of science that catapulted social constructionism into the mainstream of American intellectual thought. His account of scientific development touches on all the ideas that I have discussed so far and extends them in interesting ways.

In brief, Kuhn argues that science doesn't progress in a straightforward linear fashion. It is misleading to think that science is merely an uninterrupted chain of problem solving wherein each generation builds knowledge by focusing on unsolved puzzles. Science instead occasionally experiences rather abrupt change, what Kuhn calls a "paradigm shift." By that, Kuhn means that scientists as a group introduce a new way of seeing an area of research that is so different from the way that preceded it that science proceeds with new terms and new ideas. Between these conceptual "revolutions," researchers solve puzzles within the guidelines of the existing paradigm. Solving the "small puzzles" of everyday science does not require radical new ideas. Rather, it requires the persistent application of existing ideas.

In the language of social construction, Kuhn claims that at most times scientists working on a topic employ a very stable frame, which occasionally dissolves and is replaced by a new frame. *Structure*, then, is the story of how framings in scientific communities are established, habitualized, and occasionally replaced with new framings. The oscillation between the long periods of normal science and the eruptions of revolutionary science depends on social construction processes within the scientific community. Kuhn's central argument is not, in my reading, philosophical. He does not, for example, make any strong claims about what is and is not science (the "demarcation problem" in philosophy), nor does he make epistemic claims about how science should be done. *The Structure of Scientific Revolutions* is instead a book dedicated to various social processes. Kuhn discusses how scientists are socialized into the dominant paradigm of the day, how people begin to question the underlying assumptions of scientific theories, and how older generations of scientists view younger scientists with befuddlement. I am not claiming that *Structure* is devoid of philosophical claims, which is clearly not the case. My point is simpler: the purpose of Kuhn's work is to uncover the social and intellectual processes that drive change in scientific communities.

Here, I draw attention to the ways that Kuhn's account of science relies on arguments that are very common in social construction theory. First, the reason that scientific paradigms persist is that young scientists are socialized into them via courses and textbooks. One might argue that seminars and conferences bond the scientific community together by institutionalizing common beliefs.

Second, there is a "stock of knowledge" of the sort discussed by Berger and Luckmann. Scientists share a common knowledge of theories, experiments, and commonly encountered observations. This knowledge is formally codified not only in texts but also in informal mores, the "folk knowledge" of science, a theme emphasized by later sociological studies of science.

The truly novel feature of Kuhn's theory is that he offers a compelling explanation for social change. Social constructionist arguments normally depict a world of reproduction. The reproduction of social facts through the process of socialization, as people learn to see the world as their peers do, leaves little room for social change to occur. If there are such strong pressures for conformity, then how does social change occur at all? Kuhn offers a very simple explanation for how social change occurs, in science at least. He argues that paradigms are based on exemplars—specific observations or experiments that motivate the rest of the theory. In psychology, one has operant conditioning—using the environment to instill predictable responses in humans and animals (e.g., Pavlov's dogs). In physics, an exemplar might be an experiment that establishes that objects do fall at the same speed, even if one is heavier than the other. Using these examples, scientists build broader theories to explain a broad range of phenomena. Kuhn posits that scientists like theories that are relatively simple, explain many observations, and are fruitful in the sense that they can be used in new settings.

But no theory can adequately cover all observations. Social change occurs within the cracks of science's theoretical foundation. Some of the time one can safely ignore anomalies—observations that aren't predicted by or accounted for in the theory. Anomalies might be explained later, or they might turn out to be unimportant upon further reflection. At other times, the theory can be modified or adjusted to account for the observation. But sometimes an anomaly can't be brushed under the carpet. There is no way to discount the anomaly or otherwise draw it under the umbrella of current theory. A single anomaly won't overturn a paradigm, but many anomalies are dangerous for scientific theory because they expose the problems in a taken-for-granted theory on which the discipline rests. Over time, the problems accumulate, making it harder and harder to sustain the theory. There is widespread awareness in the community that the reigning theory is flawed. Scientists eventually decide to abandon the theory, clearing the way for a new idea, a new paradigm with its own exemplars and its own rules of science.

Kuhn's theory allows social change to happen because there is something outside the system of belief. As Karl Popper notes about science, it is possible for things to occur that were not predicted.[6] In addition, scientists, relative to other people, rigidly apply rules of reasoning. Bend the rules once, and few notice. Bend the rules many times, and you lose face. Thus, science, in Kuhn's telling, is a belief system that can be affected by external factors. The social support for the system decreases the more that the system is twisted by its adherents.

It is worth asking if Kuhn's model of paradigm shift can be expanded to areas beyond science. In some ways, it can't. Science might be unique in that open admission of error is commonplace and even encouraged. I am not claiming that individual scientists rush to admit error. Science is filled with individuals who cling to theories that are becoming outdated. I am instead claiming that science seems to be a social system where third parties are successful in arguing that predecessors were mistaken in a way that causes people to revise their views. In contrast, other belief systems, such as religions or political ideologies, seem immune to the type of change that occurs in science. Thus, one wouldn't expect change in political or religious belief systems to happen in the same way that change in science happens.

PROTEST-MOVEMENT FRAMING

Though Kuhn's text is an extremely well-known example of a constructionist argument, it was not written with sociologists in mind. In this section, I discuss applications of framing to an issue of deep concern to sociologists—protest and political contention. For many years, scholars examining riots, protest, and other forms of contention often relied on theories of "objective conditions." That is, it was commonly believed that political protest followed "real-world" material conditions.[7] According to the theory, people should protest more often during times of economic decline or if the government is actively repressing people because these situations directly harm people. A similar claim was made about other types of movements. One might think that environmental protest is more likely to happen in places with pollution or that pro-life movements should be most common in places with high abortion rates. Many movement scholars used "objective conditions" to explain when and where protest happens. This is not meant to be an overly simplistic argument about causes and effect but a recognition of the possibility that protest is often aimed at some concrete state of affairs or state policy.

But subsequent research has shown that this hypothesis is often mistaken. Numerous movements appear to have developed during times when "objective conditions" were improving or relatively good. In America, the civil rights movement crested in the 1950s and 1960s, a time of economic growth and of thawing race relations: lynchings were on the decline, millions of African

Americans escaped Jim Crow by moving North, and public opinion was slowly moving in the direction of racial tolerance.

The French Revolution seems to display a similar pattern. The grievances against the French monarchy reached a peak at a time when the economy was in relatively good condition. Many historians have documented that, contrary to popular belief, the French economy was expanding during the eighteenth century.[8] Similar anomalies can be found in other social movements. In the case of environmentalists, green movements are most likely to be found in wealthy nations that have relatively clean environments. They are less likely to be found in developing nations that have unclean technologies. The point isn't that objective conditions never matter. Certainly, whites treated blacks with much cruelty in the United States, the French monarchy was a financial disaster, and manufacturing was very dirty in many parts of the Western world. The point is that the timing of the movements doesn't coincide with the peak of these problems (e.g., antiblack violence crested in the 1920s, but the civil rights movement saw its largest mobilizations in the 1960s). These observations by themselves do not completely refute materialist views of protest movements. They instead indicate the need for additional elements of explanation.

Various explanations have been offered for the loose coupling of politics and objective conditions. A very popular theory involves framing. Promoted by the sociologist David Snow, framing theory in social movement research suggests that people will join a cause only if they have been presented with a persuasive and highly negative interpretation of events.[9] People must come to believe that they can no longer accept the current state of things, that there is a "problem" that can be resolved through political action. Environmentalism is an excellent example. Nearly all human actions create by-products that may affect or kill other organisms. However, it was only in the eighteenth and nineteenth centuries that Westerners began to feel that animals and the physical environment deserve special treatment. In the twentieth century, the mass media depicted the destruction of the environment in books such as *Silent Spring* by Rachel Carson ([1962] 2002) and popularized the view that people should act to prevent industry from damaging nature. In other words, human activity has always altered the larger biological environment, but pollution was not defined as a problem until the twentieth century.

Taking a cue from social constructionists, Snow and his collaborators have argued that social movements depend on people who frame the issue in a way that draws people together.[10] Leaders do things such as create "master frames" that tie together different issues. Movement activists engage in "frame alignment," linking different frames so they resonate with each other and the larger culture. Thus, the rise of a movement is not merely about people responding to some specific event but also about which cause is framed to resonate in the larger social environment. Movement emergence is a lengthy process where people must be persuaded that something actually is wrong. The act of persuasion must be felt within the broader culture. The framing within the movement usually must resonate with the culture in the wider society. It is for that reason that nearly every American political movement claims that the Founding Fathers would have supported their proposals.

Two examples from my own research on protest movements illustrate the importance of framing for movements. From 2004 to 2011, my collaborator (Michael T. Heaney) and I studied the movement against the U.S. war in Iraq. Starting in 2006 and ending in 2009, the antiwar movement collapsed. At its height shortly after the 2003 invasion of Iraq, the movement could reliably stage protests that attracted hundreds of thousands of people. By 2009, the movement was lucky if it could attract a few dozen people to a protest. This erosion of the antiwar movement deserves explanation because of the relative continuity in policy between the Bush and Obama administrations. The decline in troops was negotiated by George W. Bush in 2006 and carried out by Obama in 2009. Furthermore, Obama escalated the war on terror in other ways. He increased deployments in Afghanistan, used drone strikes in many Middle Eastern nations, intervened in the Libyan civil war, and, ironically, increased the number of American troops in Iraq in 2016 as a response to the rise of the Islamic State in Iraqi territory. So why did the antiwar movement disappear if Obama continued and escalated various conflicts in the Middle East? We argue that framing was a major issue. When the antiwar movement erupted in the early 2000s, both protest leaders and street protesters framed the war as a Republican issue. This framing was effective for mobilizing people, and it resulted in large numbers of Democrats attending antiwar rallies. Ironically, however, the same framing contributed to the decline of the movement. Once Democrats gained control of Congress in 2006 and the White House in 2008, many activists no longer viewed the war in such problematic terms. If political leaders were from the same party, many assumed that the war was more legitimate or that it was managed in a better way. Antiwar protest subsequently declined and has remained modest throughout the Obama administration.[11]

A second example shows how movement framing can affect whether a movement gets what it wants from those in power. Here, I draw on my own research on student protest. In the 1960s, there was a movement on American college campuses to create black studies programs, which would focus on the history and culture of African Americans. Black studies was initially framed as a remedy to campus racism. Activists claimed that college curriculum excluded black history and ideas. Later, framing played a role in how the educational establishment responded to the black studies movement. If campus activists framed black studies as a political enterprise, proposals for new programs would be rejected. For example, college deans tended to reject demands for black studies if students claimed the proposed program would promote a nationalist cultural agenda. If, however, activists could claim that black studies rested on an interdisciplinary foundation in the humanities and social sciences, proposals were more likely to be accepted. Framing also played a role in how educational administrators treated student activists. When administrators were able to frame activists as militants, they found it easy to institute rules allowing them to expel the protesters.[12] The lesson from the case of black studies and other such movements is this: framing not only affects how people see a problem and thus choose to join a movement but is also affects the vitality and success of a movement.

PERFORMATIVITY THEORY

A more radical approach to social construction theory suggests that it is possible to create our social world so that it conforms with what we think the world should look like. An early example of this, from the late 1960s, is Robert Merton's theory of the self-fulfilling prophecy. Merton noted that beliefs can accidentally cause a new state of events.[13] He used bank runs to illustrate this point. Imagine that a bank is operating with fractional reserves. That means that only a small amount of cash is retained in the bank itself, and the rest is loaned or invested. Normally, this is not a problem. On a typical day, only a small fraction of depositors will ask for cash. The problem arises when a large proportion of depositors ask for money. Because the bank has only a small amount of cash, the bank would have to shut its doors, and the bank might cease to exist. Merton's observation is that a belief about the insolvency of a bank, whether founded on fact or not, might cause the bank to become insolvent. A rumor might suggest that the bank is about to shut down, which triggers a stampede of customers, who ask for their money and cause the bank to become insolvent. The key point of the bank-run example is that the bank may have been doing business in a prudent way, but a spontaneous rumor can cause the bank to close. Beliefs create a new reality wherein rumors become self-fulfilling prophecy.

In recent years, sociologists have formulated arguments even stronger than the self-fulfilling prophecy. Performativity theory asserts that abstract theories can, under certain conditions, make the social world conform to its predictions. Donald MacKenzie's book *An Engine, Not a Camera: How Financial Models Shape the Markets* (2006) makes precisely this claim about economic theory.[14] Economic theory not only describes markets but is also a narrative that creates them.

To understand MacKenzie's argument, it helps to describe a few facts about the history and theory of financial markets. For many years, investors and economists have asked how one should price a financial instrument, such as a bond or stock. The issue is complicated. The price should not only reflect its present value but also incorporate a guess about its future performance. Some investors thought that the price should follow prior trends, a theory called "chartism" because one simply charts previous stock prices to determine the current price. However, in the 1960s and 1970s economists developed models that revolutionized the theory and practice of stock and bond pricing. One model was the efficient-market hypothesis. The idea is that stock prices already incorporate relevant information. Therefore, there is no point in trying to pick special undervalued stocks or otherwise outperform the market. Investors should instead buy a wide range of stocks to take advantage of the overall growth in the market. Another path-breaking idea is the Black–Scholes model. The idea is that prices randomly fluctuate, and the price of the stock option should reflect this randomness and the financial resources needed to buy the stock.

MacKenzie's point is not whether the efficient-market hypothesis or the Black–Scholes model is right or wrong. He focuses instead on these models' impact on financial markets. He does not assume that economic models simply describe reality; rather, he thinks that they change reality. He offers interesting examples. The efficient-market hypothesis suggests that prices should incorporate all relevant information. There should not be inexplicable price changes related to the weather or other factors. Research by financial economists, often motivated by the efficient-market hypothesis, showed was that there were inexplicable but systematic price fluctuations. Upon discovery, these anomalies were publicized, exploited by investors, and then *disappeared*. Thus, the economic theory didn't merely describe the financial market. It created a world where the theory was used to change the world so that it conformed with the theory.

So far I have described examples in which economic theory guides investors, who arbitrage away profit opportunities, but MacKenzie doesn't stop there. He argues that economic theories create new actors, new rules, and essentially a new market based on financial theories. Tools such as the Black–Scholes model and the binomial option price model were converted into computer programs that traders used to judge the observed prices. A stock option or other derivative was judged in comparison to the price predicted by various models and theories. Traders then internalized the rules of behavior that are predicted by these economic models until they became institutionalized. They bought and sold securities as if they were acting out a textbook model. In other words, the theory was used to create the people and the strategies that characterize these markets.

CONNECTIONS

There is much more to social construction theory. I only briefly delved into Erving Goffman's work and did not explore other topics that rely heavily on social construction arguments, such as the "strong program" in the sociology of science, which argues that modern sciences, such as physics, are interwoven with their social contexts. However, the discussion provided does help us understand how social construction relates to other theoretical issues in sociology. For example, Randall Collins's discussion of ritual chains lays heavy emphasis on copresence and, conversely, exclusion. This emphasis provides a concrete and direct link to theories of social inequality. As noted in chapter 2, many theories of inequality begin with the observation that inequality is maintained by excluding people from resources, which often means tangible things such as money, housing, jobs, and education. I also noted that contemporary theories of inequality focus on symbolic exclusion as well. Collins's theory emphasizes another element of stratification—the exclusion from situations where people get to determine the norms of their community. Thus, ritual-chain theory and modern stratification research possess an important point of intersection—the process of boundary creation and maintenance.

Another connection to stratification theory that merits discussion is Pierre Bourdieu's theory of symbolic violence, which describes how individuals come to accept a view of the world that entails their own domination.[15] The classic example used to illustrate this idea is gender: symbolic violence occurs when people assert that one gender is weaker than the other.[16] Theories of social construction are important because they draw attention to the issue of how people come to develop this specific gender ideology, a point not addressed in Bourdieu's original analysis but elaborated upon by later scholars. The recurring gathering of people, which may be sorted by gender, and their practices inculcates the ideology of gender, which contributes to the discrimination practiced by men as well as to the repressive ideology of women's inferiority.

A different connection to other branches of sociological theory is the debate over individual action in institutionalism. Critics often claim institutional theories focus too much on conformity and constraint and not enough on individual action. A lot of iron cage but not much individual action. The various theories presented in this chapter provide ample examples in which individuals can resist the sorts of pressures described by institutionalists because they are always interpreting or adding meaning to the practices that are part of the ritual chain. That is, the actors in current social construction theories don't passively enact norms. They shape them. The scientist in Kuhn's account of scientific change questions the efficacy of a paradigm; the activist tries to resist the dominant framing of social problems. Although the reliance on interaction is an appealing way to think about social life, it doesn't address institutionalism's main observation—that social life seems, at times, to be very regulated. Collins's theory only partially addresses this issue. Ritual chains might lead to conformity, or they might not. It is entirely possible that as rituals and social practices are reproduced, they change in ways that lead to social diversity. Consider the world of music. Even though music is organized by ritual chains (bands and concerts are connected through time), we live in a world of astounding musical diversity. What is needed is an account of social aggregation that employs some of the basic language of social construction but specifies the conditions leading to uniformity and other conditions where diversity is achieved.

A final connection worth noting is the link between social construction theory and rational action. A good starting point is Émile Durkheim's observation about morals and markets—economic behavior requires a moral framework, trust between participants.[17] People need to understand what is permissible and expected in a market situation and what they can expect from each other. There needs to be a shared framework that will allow people to cooperate. What Durkheim hints at in his comment is that decision making usually follows a sense-making process. In other words, every decision relies on social construction of what the options are. People rely on the "stock of knowledge" about their situation to determine how they will act. We can return here to an example from an earlier chapter. The decision to attend college is not merely a weighing of costs and benefits but also a *perception* of the costs. People at home, with their families, develop beliefs about what college is actually about, and a constructionist approach to college enrollment would delve into exactly how this process works.

• • •

Social construction has been a focal point of sociology since the foundation of the discipline because social construction is what normally happens when people meet. What do we believe? What is the world like, and what do we need to do in that world? These are the questions that all groups answer if they are to have any identity at all. This process of determining how people collectively perceive reality and act upon these perceptions can be analyzed with respect to a few key processes and mechanisms—the creation of repeated interactions, the use of frames to define situations and coordinate people, and the creation of facts, which are transmitted to future group members through socialization. In turn, these processes speak to other issues such as inequality, social change, and instrumental action. Though social construction may be the last topic that is discussed in this book, it is by no means the least important, and it can claim to stand on equal footing with the other major topics of sociology.

6

COMBINING DIFFERENT THEORIES

FROM INGREDIENTS TO COMBINATIONS

THIS book explains how contemporary sociologists create their explanations of social life. The purpose of reviewing the various studies in this book is that they reveal sociology's playbook, the recipes or intellectual "moves" commonly used by sociologists. The recipe ingredients are mechanisms, the processes that link social outcomes together. But as any musician or chef will tell you, great art doesn't emerge from the rigid application of rules and recipes. Rather, learning the rules of art imbues fluency and a mastery of technique, which can be used to create something new and insightful. Sociology is no different. Models are just models. They need to be adjusted, modified, and combined in new ways that reflect the way researchers understand social life. Indeed, much of the research covered in this book does precisely that. The progress of modern sociology comes from reformulating or modifying the ideas presented by earlier generations of social scientists.

This final chapter focuses on the merging or synthesis of the different mechanisms presented in this book. Much of the vibrancy of sociology comes from combining perspectives that at first might seem disparate or incompatible. One might think of this process as creating a sort of collage of views, looking for insight by mixing heterogeneous things together, but that is not an accurate analogy. Rather, sociologists have come to appreciate the richness of social life. An interaction might be guided by a frame, as suggested by Erving Goffman's theory, but it doesn't mean that there is nothing purposive or strategic about the people who are interacting with each other. It can be very informative to consider how individual choices might be shaped by framing.

I conclude the book here with a discussion of social theory that resonates in sociology because of its ability to pull together different types of social explanation. I start by revisiting Pierre Bourdieu. In chapter 2, I presented the French sociologist's work as a generalization of or sequel to classical Marxist theories. Instead of seeing class struggle as the primary form of social conflict, Bourdieu moved to a theory that depicted society as a struggle for status, but status can come in many forms. This discussion of synthetic social theories starts with a closer look at aspects of Bourdieu's work that I downplayed earlier, such as its lesser-noted reliance on social construction and strategic action. Then I focus on two writers who have received very little attention in sociology so far, even though they have had an indisputable impact on it—Michel Foucault and Judith Butler. I discuss their analysis of sexuality because of how they employ classic social construction arguments while integrating them with classical and modern approaches to social inequality.

This chapter then investigates a different type of example of strategic-action research that draws from ideas associated with other types of sociology—Michael Chwe's analysis of social ritual. The essence of Chwe's argument is that social life requires coordination and that people do things to create the knowledge needed for coordination. But unlike the functionalists of seventy years ago, Chwe does not assume that norms will automatically lead to the creation of a common body of knowledge. He uses rational-choice arguments to explain the specific conditions that must occur for common knowledge to emerge.

Finally, I spend some time discussing how a reader might carry out such an eclectic approach, by way of the example of how people are interpreting genetic data that they can now obtain from doctors and self-testing. A number of sociologists have observed that the use of such data triggers discussion not only of health but of race as well. Thus, the analysis requires a discussion of the construction of medical knowledge and of how racial differences are created and reproduced.

I chose to look specifically at the authors discussed here because they employ multiple styles of argument instead of a single mechanism. They all strive to bring together different dimensions of social life. Mechanisms are linked and sometimes nested within each other. As well as offering insights, the theories these authors present have resonance because they bridge ideas that might be seen as incompatible.

BOURDIEU: SOCIAL CONSTRUCTIONIST MEETS INEQUALITY THEORIST

I start by looking at Pierre Bourdieu, whom we already encountered in chapter 2. In that chapter, Bourdieu is presented as a theorist of social power and inequality. People acquire status by successfully playing the game of their "social field." This is a fruitful way to approach his work because it captures one reason that Bourdieu's writings have retained their interest among sociologists—their ability to capture the creation and reproduction of status in an allegedly egalitarian society. The theory of fields and habitus provides a much-needed generalization of the arguments about inequality found among previous students of social class, such as Marx and Weber. But this thumbnail sketch does not exhaust Bourdieu's work. Other aspects of his thought reveal connections to the other ideas in this book, such as social constructionism and cultural sociology. In combination with his basic insights about inequality, these strands have helped Bourdieu's works shape the mainstream of contemporary sociology.

Bourdieu's most well-known book is probably *Distinction: A Sociological Critique of Taste* (1984), a study that examines French citizens' cultural taste. In *Distinction*, Bourdieu makes a simple but powerful argument about social class and consumption. What people eat, the movies they see, even the pictures they put on their walls reflect their class position in society. The essence of class distinction is not only that wealthy people can afford more things (they can) or that wealthier people can afford nicer versions of things (also true). It is that upper-class people, working-class people, and middle-class people want different things. In support of this point, Bourdieu conducted interviews with French citizens, collected data about the types of leisure activities in which they participate and what they consumed, and even took photographs of their residences. The differences were simple but telling. Upper-class people had more of a "highbrow" taste focusing on the fine arts. Middle-class people had "middlebrow" taste— watching movies that required more from the audience but were not rooted in classical culture. Lower-class people preferred films rooted in popular culture. This sort of stratification of preferences was reflected across many types of consumption.

What is important for the present discussion is how Bourdieu subtly ties his analysis of class as habitus to other concerns of sociology. From the perspective of the social constructionist, habitus is the culmination of these patterns of consumption that reflect the attempt to establish class boundaries. How we construct the social world is intimately tied to our relative status. The way we criticize lower-income people who purchase luxury goods reveals a strategy by which we further define our own status while denigrating others. Watching a Shakespeare play isn't only about enjoying the Bard's works; it is about signaling to others and to oneself that one is a wealthy and educated person.

There are other links between Bourdieu's work and the other ideas covered in this book. For example, habitus and its attendant consumption patterns might be interpreted as a "cultural tool kit." What one consumes is a way to acquire necessary goods, but it is also based on a menu of strategies that emerge from a very specific social environment. Ann Swidler was rather open about where these tool kits come from. The original tool kit article indicates they might come from growing up in a specific nation.[1] The book *Habits of the Heart* contains examples of Americans who are drawing on American culture.[2] The man who justifies his drive for income might appeal to the ideology of individualism.

Bourdieu's contribution to the discussion of tool kits and their origins is the idea that these tool kits may be rooted in social class to a degree underappreciated in other writings. Indeed, an entire cottage industry of sociology has sprung up to examine how it is exactly that people acquire these class-based consumption patterns and if these patterns change over time. For example, Shamus Khan's ethnography of an elite boarding school argues that modern upper-class people cultivate a relaxed cosmopolitanism, an ability to enjoy a wide range of cultural goods.[3] In earlier generations, the habitus of the social elite was characterized by having very specific tastes, such as an appreciation for the opera or high French cuisine. Now people from privileged backgrounds consume everything—they are "omnivores." The Ivy League graduate can appreciate both opera and hip-hop, and he or she is just as likely to eat greasy hamburgers as sushi. Khan uses his time spent at an elite boarding school to examine how exactly these omnivorous choices are cultivated. He spends time with students as they learn from other students and faculty how to "hang out" with others of different backgrounds and to display an air of ease and confidence in all situations. Furthermore, he explains why such attitudes are important in the modern economy. The business and political leaders of the future must be able to easily access various fields of knowledge and power. An executive must learn to interact with other executives, the engineers who create a firm's products, the political elites who can affect a firm's financial future, as well as the workers who perform the firms' more mundane nuts-and-bolts tasks. The cultivated air of the omnivore is part of a habitus that is well suited to the modern world, and exclusive schools are the places where this habitus is forged. Thus, in studies such as Khan's, Swidler's cultural tool kit meets the class-based status seeker of Bourdieu's habitus and field theory.

THE POST-STRUCTURAL APPROACH TO SEXUALITY

A literature that I call the "post-structural approach to sexuality" is a prime example of how authors have combined theories. I have previously discussed some of these authors, such as Michel Foucault, but not others, such as Judith Butler and Eve Sedgwick. What these authors have in common is a view of gender and sexuality that combines social constructionism and theories of power, a view that was uncommon among academics before the 1980s. I use the term *post-structural* because their writings followed, appropriated, and critiqued authors who were labeled "structuralist," such as Marx and Freud.[4] Though not strictly sociological in the sense of building on the traditions of Durkheim or Weber, the post-structural theory of sexuality has had a strong impact on the subfield of sociology that addresses how people identify themselves through their sexual orientation or gender.

A good starting point for this discussion is Foucault's multivolume work *The History of Sexuality*.[5] The general purpose of this text is to argue against the common belief that the Industrial Revolution brought about a suppression of sex. Foucault insists that he does not deny the fact that sexual practices are often regulated and controlled. Rather, the insistence on Victorian prudishness draws attention away from the proliferation of sexual discussions in Western nations and the rise of modern social categories such as "homosexuals" and "heterosexuals" that did not exist in earlier epochs. Thus, *The History of Sexuality* is an exploration of how people defined sexual categories, how these categories became an integral part of one's identity, and why Western people came to believe that they were a sexually repressive society in the nineteenth century.

The History of Sexuality combines two themes that inform Foucault's thinking. We already encountered one of these themes in chapter 2: how power is created in Western society. From the perspective of mechanisms, the organizing principle of this book, Foucault asks us to believe that modernity was propelled by a type of socialization where people learned to punish themselves and by the creation of institutions that enabled dominant groups to monitor and imprison low-status groups. *The History of Sexuality* is an examination of one aspect of social control—the regulation of human sexuality. Foucault discusses the many ways that law and social custom were marshaled to control sexual behavior. The other theme is the social construction of sexuality. Much of *The History of Sexuality* is actually a historical overview of how different

Western intellectuals viewed sexuality. He examines how writers from ancient Greece to the Middle Ages to the Renaissance and so on to modern times discussed sex and developed a general theory of what is acceptable behavior. According to Foucault, over the centuries intellectuals slowly redefined nonnormative sexual behavior into a type, or "species," of person, who was then subject to medical and legal regulation. Thus, to link how sexuality was regulated in early Europe to how it is regulated in later periods, one must develop a mechanism of socialization wherein people develop new ideas about proper or legitimate sexuality and then explain how people were socialized into this new view.

Foucault notes that the Greeks and other writers in antiquity did not seem to possess the concepts that we now use to regulate sexual behavior. Though the ancients did frequently talk of sex, they did not have the modern view that sex should be controlled or suppressed. Classical writers did not have the view that homosexuals, for example, were a distinct class of people who should be the target of government regulation. They instead engaged in a series of debates about the issues regarding the nature of pleasure and how one can control one's passions. For classical writers, according to Foucault, the issue was how one could fashion a moral attitude or approach to sexual experiences, not how the state should regulate sexual acts. "Putting it schematically, we could say that classical antiquity's moral reflection was not directed toward a codification of acts, nor toward a hermeneutics of the subject, but toward a stylization of attitudes and an aesthetics of existence."[6] Thus, ancient writers were concerned about how one could resist passions and maintain control over oneself. They did not consider how the government could be used to prohibit sexual practice or promote specific orientations.

Thus, the "truth" of sex among the Greeks and the Romans was produced via philosophical discourse. What is different in modern society is that what we believe to be true about sex, beginning especially in the early-modern era, is produced via a *scientia sexualis*, a technical discourse developed by doctors and scientists. Foucault notes the performative aspect of this discourse. Doctors in the eighteenth and nineteenth centuries would build theaters, places of demonstration, where they would hold lectures and educate the public about their discoveries. The *scientia sexualis* is often based on a ritual of confession, where people with all manner of sexual behavior and preference offer up their experiences. The parallel with torture is not lost on Foucault. Having people confess their sexuality to scientists produces medical knowledge in much the same way that torturing prisoners creates political knowledge.

Here we can see how Foucault merges social construction arguments with arguments about power. It is not possible to assert social power without an ability to define the "target." In a much earlier era, people simply were not concerned about homosexuals as an identifiable class of people. In the early-modern era, however, physicians began to spend much time trying to impose a uniform view of heterosexual sex and trying to classify and analyze "deviants." The scientific construction of an identity became widespread, which then enabled more systematic legal regulation of sex and eventually persecution of nonheterosexuals. Thus, social construction enabled the creation of social power.

Next, we can turn to Judith Butler's analysis of sexuality.[7] Like Foucault, Butler is interested in the construction of sexuality, but her work differs in some crucial ways. Unlike Foucault, she is not invested in exploring the intellectual history of sexuality. Her analysis does not review classical and modern authors and only occasionally mentions the laws surrounding sexuality. She instead offers a cultural analysis of sexuality that emphasizes its performative nature. The core of Butler's argument is that sexual identity and gender are performances of the sort Goffman describes in *The Presentation of the Self in Everyday Life* (1959). That is, there is no "core" notion of or eternal truth regarding what straight or gay people should be like. Rather, what they "should" be like is something that is defined and asserted during interaction.

Butler's arguments go beyond the observation that sexual identities must be performed. Butler goes on to assert that sexual identities have a cutting, campy aspect. She suggests that heterosexual ideals of beauty represent an exaggeration of what people might find attractive. Women are often encouraged to vastly exaggerate their appearance, and men are expected to overemphasize their physical strength. Although this correlation was noted earlier, Butler's insight is that gay identities are often derivative in the sense that they are appropriations of already over-the-top straight performances. Consider, for example, the trope that gay men are supposed to be attracted to extremely masculinized men. In this, the expression of same-sex attraction utilizes the stereotype of straight men as overly muscular.

To this observation, Butler and others have added the argument that these sexual performances are integrated into other structures of society. For example, the expectation in most societies so far is that political leaders must be heterosexual. It is exceedingly rare that an elected official in high office presents himself or herself as being in a same-sex relationship. When it is suggested that historical figures might have been homosexual, there is often scandal, as when historian C. A. Tripp recently argued that Abraham Lincoln might have been gay.[8] In 2014, Tim Cook, the current leader of Apple, publicly acknowledged that he was in a same-sex relationship. Even though his sexual orientation had been well known for years, the public statement was newsworthy, indicating that people still expect economic leaders to be heterosexual.

The presumption that leaders are heterosexual signals a more pervasive process that contemporary scholars call "heteronormativity."[9] Roughly speaking, heteronormativity indicates that people assume that the behaviors, tastes, and attitudes of heterosexuals are normal and unremarkable, whereas those of homosexuals and other sexual minorities are deviant, unusual, confusing, and distasteful. The theory of heteronormativity shares much in common with the theory of racial privilege discussed in chapter 2. One group, heterosexuals, enjoys the benefits of its status because it follows the social standard by which others are judged. Others who don't meet this standard are treated in ways that range from disrespect to neglect to outright hostility. Although theories of racial privilege and heteronormativity have many similarities, they differ in one way that deserves commentary. Racial privilege is not discussed as a process leading to racial homogeneity, whereas heteronormativity is a situation that encourages the suppression of sexual diversity.

Racial privilege, as presented by Eduardo Bonilla-Silva and others,[10] is a process where one group enjoys the benefits of their status while at the same time denying that others are suffering from disadvantage. For example, if there are differences between blacks and whites in the completion of college, people deny that blacks have any disadvantage due to racism and insist that differences are due mainly to personal deficiencies. The argument is that black/white differences remain but emerge only from individual-level variation. In contrast, the types of processes described by heteronormativity theorists exhibit a different character. For example, one aspect of heteronormativity is that many people simply don't consciously think about other types of sexuality. Another dimension of heteronormativity is that queer identities are often suppressed or removed from the arts, education, and public discussion. Unchallenged, heteronormative culture asks that homosexuals and other sexual minorities remain silent, if not disappear altogether.

COORDINATING TOGETHER

The last two examples of sociological theory were chosen because of their popularity within sociology. They were also chosen because they serve a specific purpose—to illustrate how social explanations combine the intuitions of two or more traditions of sociology. I now discuss an example of social science, Michael Chwe's theory of social ritual, that synthesizes two topics that rarely go together: rational-choice theory and social constructionism. This synthesis is important to consider because it shows the richness of sociological thought. It also reminds us that it can be valuable to cross intellectual boundaries.

Michael Chwe is an economist who specializes in game theory—the study of how people strategically interact with each other. The main innovation of game theory is understanding that strategies are interdependent. What I do depends on what my enemy does. For example, let's say that I am a soccer player, and I have been chosen to take a penalty kick. I do not kick straight into the net because the goalie tends to stand in the middle of the net. So what most professional soccer players do is kick it to the side of the net. But what side should I kick to—the left or the right? If the kick is always to the left, the goalie will always jump there and block the shot. Likewise, constantly kicking to the right means that the goalie will know which direction to move and block the shot. The optimal thing to do—the strategy that will maximize the probability that I will score—is to randomly choose a side. Game theory is the study of how choices are connected to each other and how in some cases people will mix and match their strategies.

Not surprisingly, game theory is one of the rare tools of economics that has currency among sociologists because it is supple enough to describe the things that sociologists like to think about. One can easily imagine an election as a game where each candidate responds to the policy positions of the other candidate. One can also imagine a game where people try to gain the upper hand in an argument. In chapter 3, Richard Breen and John Goldthorpe's analysis of college education is presented as a sequence of decisions, which is a basic feature of game theory. The reader can easily provide examples of other social interactions that have rules that encourage people to strategically choose their actions in response to each other's choices and actions. Chwe's contribution has been to think about how game theory can be used to study the types of interaction that typically attract the attention of sociologists. Specifically, he uses game theory to analyze social rituals.

The core of Chwe's analysis is the idea that society needs to solve the problem of coordination.[11] That is, people are constantly faced with the problem of working together. I meet a professor at a conference, and he suggests that we work on a project. Should I accept? If so, what rules do we set up when we begin our project? Society is filled with all kinds of coordination problems from the mundane to the epic. At the high school dance, how will the young women and men decide on the right kind of dance? During a wave of protest, how do we get millions of people to march at the same time and demand the same thing?

Chwe, like earlier theorists, observes that "let's make some rules" is an incomplete answer to the problem of coordination. To do that, one needs to solve the problem of coordinating to have a meeting to make the rules. Obviously, it's not adequate to say that we need a meeting to decide how we will have a meeting to settle the rules! The way around this logical problem is to inject common knowledge into society. In other words, if we could just go into each person's mind and give him or her the knowledge for how to cooperate with others, people would cooperate with each other.

Chwe's argument is that rituals serve that function in society. They are meetings of people where they learn something about how society works and, more importantly, where they learn that *other people* know the rules. Rituals bypass the common-knowledge problem. People don't form their own understandings of society but instead are gathered together in a ritual and told how society works. Once the ritual is done, people possess the common knowledge needed for interaction. Rituals are a game that has the right rules that will let people work together in everyday life.

The theory is illustrated with a series of interesting examples. One example is the shape of theaters in early and modern societies. It is very common for theaters to have circular shapes so as to reinforce that the whole group is exposed to the same knowledge. Committee meeting rooms in corporations and universities often have this circular shape as well. Chwe also uses data from advertising to show that products with a communal character (beer, for example) have larger advertising budgets because firms that sell these social goods need to inform a larger number of people about the product. He also revisits a favorite example of twentieth-century social theory that we visited in chapter 2—the panopticon. In Foucault's telling, the panopticon was an instrument of discipline and invisible monitoring. Chwe goes back to Jeremy Bentham's original description. He finds that the panopticon did have the central tower that was used to watch prisoners, but it also had a chapel, which was meant to provide a focus for observance. The panopticon was, contrary to Foucault, not merely a machine dream of discipline but also, to a certain extent, a tool for creating a common culture among prisoners.

It helps to compare Chwe's account with that of sociologists who think about social rituals and common knowledge. For example, Chwe himself argues against the view that rituals serve their integration function because of emotional resonance, as Randall Collins argues. His argument shares something in common with Peter Berger and Thomas Luckmann's arguments but diverges in important ways. Both Chwe and Berger and Luckmann acknowledge that common knowledge is a prerequisite for society, but they disagree on how that knowledge is formed. Berger and Luckmann offer the mechanism of "habitualization." People meet in small groups over time. Each time they meet, they revise and refine their expectations. Once these expectations are learned by an ever-increasing number of people, they become "common knowledge" or "institutionalized." In contrast, Chwe suggests that it is literally impossible for order to emerge in this way and that common knowledge must be introduced via exogenous shocks— that is, rituals. In this view, Chwe shares much with theorists such as Jeffrey Alexander who link social integration with public rituals. Chwe sees ritual simply as matter of information, not culture or the ways that people interpret the world. The mechanisms that transform a mass of uncoordinated people into a real society are the ritual and the imparting of common knowledge in ritual.

There has been much debate over the merits of Chwe's theory of ritual, but it remains important because it is a bridge between sociology and other types of social science, such as economics. Chwe even cites Goffman, one of the leading figures of twentieth-century sociology, who said that game theory might illuminate culture, and Claude Lévi-Strauss, who suggested that game theory would allow for the "increasing consolidation of social anthropology, economics, and linguistics into one great field, that of communication."[12] Chwe's text suggests one way that this meeting of fields might occur.

DOING IT YOURSELF: GENETIC TESTING AND RACE

There is much to be gained from reviewing the great social scientists and how they mix and match explanations, but that is not the primary goal of this chapter or the book. Rather, I want you, the reader, to be able to apply various ideas to new social phenomena that they encounter and to do so in a flexible way that draws upon the multiple streams of social thought found in this book. Not only will this synthesis illuminate a specific issue in your mind, but it will also expand sociological theory itself as people's intuitions encounter new social phenomena and must be revised. But how should you carry out this synthesis and evolution of theory? I suggest the following. First, recognize that social phenomena often have multiple components. Social behaviors often reflect inequality in society: they reflect the choices people make; they reflect people's interpretations of events; and they reflect institutions and their values. Ask yourself a few questions, such as how people interpret a specific thing and how they use that interpretation to achieve their goals. Second, it is often quite helpful to focus on one or two aspects of the phenomena and then ask how one aspect shapes the other. Such connections are often not hard to find. When we look at society, we often see people openly discussing or disputing the issues that feature so prominently in this book. One may see such debates as a "smoke signal" for social processes that deserve more attention.

A recent development in modern society illustrates these principles: the appearance of low-cost genetic testing through services such as 23andMe for the purposes of discovering ancestry or managing the risk of disease associated with certain genes. Here, we can choose one of the major themes of the book and examine how it relates to another with reference to genetic testing.

For example, one of the major lessons of social constructionism is that people must develop a frame and interpretation for most of what they do. Not surprisingly, there have been many discussions of exactly what that means. Understanding the social meaning of DNA tests is crucial to understanding how that technology affects inequality and institutions, two other themes in the book. The philosopher Ian Hacking notes that the meaning and value of genes is up for grabs. In some cases, genetic information is used to manage personal risk or to make a point about paternity or to make racial claims.[13] Technology isn't "obvious"; it has to be interpreted.

Alondra Nelson makes the social meaning of genetic information the focus of her recent book, *The Social Life of DNA: Race, Reparations, and Reconciliation After the Genome* (2016). Nelson discusses the many ways that inexpensive genetic testing is making an appearance in racial discussions. For example, some African Americans are using the outcomes of DNA testing to create stronger ties with potential relatives in Africa. Some people don't know whether they have African ancestors who may or may not have been slaves. Others want to know which area of Africa their ancestors may come from and long for a sense of comity with them. Nelson calls the responses to the taking of these DNA tests "reconciliation projects," which attempt to atone for historical traumas by bringing people together by means of genetic data. Thus, one can see how a social construction process is the mechanism that leads to changes in racial inequalities. If genetic data are interpreted as relevant to the issue of community and ancestry, then one can use the data to convince others that they belong to the same community. If genetic data is brought into a legal and political context, it may be used to bridge the economic gap between whites and blacks in the United States.

This thumbnail sketch of how DNA testing intervenes into racial discourse is enough to emphasize an important point. One can construct plausible mechanisms for social change first by recognizing that the basic elements of inequality, choice, institutions, and social construction often appear in most social situations and then by asking how these elements relate to each other. The challenge, therefore, is to develop explanations that are coherent, supported by the data, and speak to these broad themes of sociology.

•　•　•

This book has a single goal. I want people to understand the main themes of sociological theory and apply them to what they see in the world. Helping them do so can be accomplished in an accessible way that relates long-standing theoretical discussions to modern empirical research. Mechanisms are my tool for achieving that goal because, ultimately, most students of the social sciences really want to know how we get from X to Y in our explanations. If your purpose in reading this book is to see what my discipline is about, I thank you for your patience and pray that you come away with a positive impression. If you are a sociologist, then I hope that I have helped you achieve some clarity about how the discipline is organized and, maybe, figure out where you might be going next.

EPILOGUE

BOOKS are written for many reasons. This book is my attempt to understand what sociology is all about. Sociology is too often depicted as a chaotic, often anarchic discipline. The casual observer might justifiably infer that anything is permitted in sociology. That same casual observer might also think that there is no intellectual structure to sociology because there is no dominant school of thought, and basic texts vary a great deal in what they cover. Upon beginning my graduate studies in sociology, I, too, bought into the Tower of Babel view of sociology. There was nothing in my graduate education that led me to believe otherwise. Most sociology graduate programs have required courses in classical social theory, but they are not directly connected to current research. The elective courses may or may not build on earlier courses.

My views changed when I began teaching. In 2004, my department chair asked if I could teach the required undergraduate course on social theory. I was also teaching a first-year graduate course that introduced students to the "macro" issues in modern sociology. I relied on textbooks for undergraduate social theory and my own intuition of sociology for the graduate seminar. I found that my "professional" sociology course did not match up with the undergraduate course. During my doctoral education and afterward, I had developed an intuition about how sociology was intellectually organized, so that is what I taught to graduate students. I also had read some scholarly analyses showing that sociological research tends to cluster into a few broad topics, such as inequality or social change. That latent structure of the discipline was most likely not on the minds of my undergraduate students, judging by the contents of the courses they were taking. That is why I wrote this book. I wanted to show people the underlying logic of sociology in a way that would be accessible to anyone who wants to know what sociology is about.

In writing this book, I also came to appreciate that sociology is pluralistic. It is a community that accepts multiple forms of analysis. Certainly, this acceptance is due in part to the type of person who is attracted to sociology. The scholar of society should be interested in both the rich and the poor, the pious and the atheist, the chaste and the promiscuous. That depth of interest isn't the only reason why sociology is a discipline of intellectual pluralism, however. I think there is a deeper reason: social life itself can't be boiled down to single thing.

But why is social life complex? I think there are three reasons. One is that human beings are governed by emotions designed to help them survive and thrive within groups. Complex situations lead to complex people. A second reason is aggregation. Humans build sophisticated social systems that have a life of their own. This does not mean that social life is immune to analysis. Rather, like a complex biological system, it will grow and develop in unexpected ways even if it still must obey some general rules. That is why some people are tool makers, some are power wielders, and others are traders and community builders. Third, people add meaning to the world and thus change it. Rocks don't decide that the world is unfair or that they want a separate society of special rocks. They're just rocks. In contrast, the meanings people assign to the world change the world, an inherently messy process.

We should therefore expect that theory should be pluralist but have some sort of intelligible foundation. Sometimes it helps to focus on social inequality, while at other times we might focus on structure and stability. When we do this, we will come up with ideas well suited to a specific feature of social life. Collectively, though, we will produce theory that settles on major topics and develops on parallel tracks. As sociology matures, people will begin to synthesize and integrate the different streams of the discipline. That has already happened in my research area, the interaction of protest and organizations (e.g., how colleges respond to student protest). Social conflict and organizational behavior were previously considered separate. People didn't see the connection between the people marching on the White House and Wall Street executives. Now it is clear that these groups are two parts of a more complex social process. As the study of protest and the study of administrative behavior have come together, it is now realized that both the building and regulation of markets and the protest within markets and governments are about framing (i.e., social construction) and rule making (e.g., institutional analysis). This merging of topics and a deeper appreciation of common social processes are happening more and more in my field, and both are very exciting. I hope that this book will help its readers understand this new sociological world.

NOTES

PREFACE

1. For example, many of the field's most popular texts start out by covering the "great classical sociologists," most of whom are men from the late nineteenth and early twentieth centuries. Charles Lemert's anthology *Social Theory: The Multicultural and Classic Readings* (2010) starts with long sections on Karl Marx, Émile Durkheim, Max Weber, and Sigmund Freud, with a few short sections on Jane Addams, George Simmel, and others. *Classical Social Theory* (2012), edited by Craig Calhoun and others, also starts with an extensive section on political and social thinkers such as Alexis de Toqueville, Marx, and Durkheim. In *Sociological Theory* (2008), George Ritzer spends the first 187 pages on the four most popular classical sociologists, Marx, Durkheim, Weber, and Simmel.

2. I studied for my sociology PhD at the University of Chicago, where I was exposed to Great Man sociology. At Chicago, we took a one-quarter social theory course in which each of the four major classical theorists received about two to three weeks of attention. This course, at the time, was taught by religion scholar Martin Riesebrodt, who was heavily indebted to the sociology of Max Weber. I also enrolled in a course taught by Don Levine, who was a preeminent student of Simmel and responsible for editing a highly influential anthology of Simmel's texts (*Georg Simmel on Individuality and Social Forms* [Simmel 1971]). Interestingly, Levine's greatest contribution to the history of social theory is a book that dispenses with Great Man sociology,

Visions of the Sociological Tradition (1995). *Visions* approaches theory in terms of national traditions rather than seminal thinkers. This approach is broadly consistent with a trend in the sociology of knowledge that situates intellectuals within an evolving network of scholars and thinkers, as in *The Sociology of Philosophies* by Randall Collins (2000).

3. Lounsbury and Carberry 2005.

4. Ritzer's (2008) text is an excellent example of this genre. The first section presents an abbreviated Great Man sociology, but the remaining 477 pages are a parade of sociological topics, including liquid modernity, Hegelian Marxism, Harold Garfinkle's ethnomoethodology, and Michael Hardt and Antonio Negri's attack on neoliberalism. This accounting does not include appendices on Michel Bourdieu, Thomas Kuhn's theory of scientific development, and micro/macrodebates. An encyclopedic source is useful but can be overwhelming for many readers, especially those with an empirical bent. A secondary criticism of this approach is that these books historically tend to overemphasize critical European theory. They oddly don't address topics that are part and parcel of mainstream empirical sociology, such as marriage, residential segregation, and religious affiliation.

5. For the socialization theory, see Lareau 2003. For the cost–benefit theory, see Breen and Goldthorpe 1997.

6. For example, the social theory books by Ritzer (2008), Lemert (2010), and Calhoun et al. (2012) have sections on globalization.

7. For the highly cited world-systems theory, see Wallerstein 1979.

8. For example, see Parsons's books *The Structure of Social Action* (1937), *The Social System* (1951), and *The Evolution of Societies* (1977).

9. See Hamilton 1991 for dozens of explanations, applications, and refutations of Parsonsian sociology. Philip Selznick (1961) accused Parsons of building a tower of words and offered an unusually dismissive review of Parsons's theory.

10. AGIL theory suggested that the sociologists needed to explain how a community Adapts to its environment, sets and achieves Goals, maintains structure though Latent functions, and manages to encourage cooperation through social Integration.

11. For simplicity, I use the terms *behavior* and *patterns of behavior* as interchangeable. When I intend to describe how an individual or an institution behaves, I make that clear in the text. If I require the specific

meaning of "pattern of behavior" within a group of community—different people with specific roles or social positions doing things in a prescribed way—then I make that clear in the text as well.

12. Probably the most popular recent exposition of this position is Gross 2009.

13. Ibid.

14. I explore the claim that sociological theories of race, class, and gender employ similar ideas and offer similar explanations in greater detail in chapter 3. For one extended treatment, see Healey 2011.

15. For a recent survey of the strengths and weaknesses of a theory of mechanisms, see Demeulenaere 2011.

16. The classic statement of sociology as incoherent is probably Alvin Gouldner's book *The Coming Crisis of Western Sociology* (1980). A more recent statement of this argument is Bernard Phillips's book *Beyond Sociology's Tower of Babel: Reconstructing the Scientific Method* (2001).

17. Roemer 1986.

18. Udry 2000 is a very well-cited example of a study within the sociology of gender that uses information about biomarkers to test theories of sex-typed behaviors. More recent examples include Cohen-Bendahan, van de Beek, and Berenbaum 2005 as well as Guo, Roettger, and Cai 2008.

19. Feyerabend 1993:14.

20. In the mid–twentieth century, a number of influential sociologists tried to compare their theories to Marxism along these lines—see, for example, Randall Collins, *Four Sociological Traditions* (1983); Lew Coser, *The Functions of Social Conflict* (1956); and Ralf Dahrendorf, *Class and Class Conflict in Modern Society* (1969).

21. For example, some scholars claim that men monopolize opportunities for pay and promotion in firms.

22. An often cited example of this theoretical strategy is W. E. B. Du Bois's discussion of white privilege in the American South ([1935] 1992:346–347).

1. WHAT COUNTS AS SOCIAL THEORY FOR THIS BOOK?

1. U.S. Census Bureau 2012.

2. Lareau 2003.

3. DiMaggio 1982.

4. Craig 2005:13–14.
5. For a discussion of the split between analytical and continental philosophers, see Gross 2002.
6. This theory was developed in its modern form by Paul Samuelson in *Foundations of Economic Analysis* ([1947] 1983).
7. A classic example of behavior economics is Daniel Kahneman and Amos Tversky's (1979) article on prospect theory; for a summary of Austrian economics, see Ludwig von Mises's book *Human Action* (1949).
8. Abend 2008.
9. See Hedström and Swedberg 1998.
10. Gross 2009:364.
11. See chapter 1 of James Coleman's book *The Foundations of Social Theory* (1990).
12. Merton 1968:39.
13. Ibid.:68.
14. For that discussion, see Lin 2002 and Portes 1998.
15. For resource mobilization theory, see McCarthy and Zald 1977.

2. POWER AND INEQUALITY

1. Loewen 2005.
2. Harlan 1968:19.
3. Ibid. Harlan's description of black schools as small, poorly maintained, single-room schools accurately captures the poor conditions at the time.
4. Woodson 1990.
5. Tolnay, Deane, and Beck 1996.
6. Du Bois 1992.
7. For example, see Lemert 2010 and Weber 2010.
8. See, for example, Connell 1987. R. W. Connell's text is a classic example of an account of gender that places emphasis on the state and rights. For a more comprehensive view of women and their legal rights in a global context, see Cook 1994.
9. The *Wall Street Journal* updates yearly law school enrollments; see, for instance, *Wall Street Journal* 2012. The Association of American Medical Colleges (2013) also has shown very large increases in the enrollment of women in medical college, with women accounting for 47 percent of recent med students.

10. For racial disparities in income, see Blau and Graham 1990; for racial disparities in health, see Williams and Mohammed 2009.
11. Du Bois [1935] 1992.
12. Rubin 1975.
13. See Frazier 1997.
14. See, for example, Carby 1997.
15. P. Collins 1990:101.
16. Mullings and Wali 2000.
17. Ibid.:163–164.
18. Terriquez 2015.
19. Chun, Lipsitz, and Shin 2013.
20. The discussion of habitus, field, and capital in this section are drawn from *An Outline of a Theory of Social Practice* (Bourdieu 1977) and *The Logic of Practice* (Bourdieu 1990b).
21. For an extensive review of voters and their inconsistent and poorly informed preferences, see Caplan 2007.
22. Brennan and Lomasky 1977.
23. Bourdieu 1998.
24. Bourdieu 1990a.
25. Bourdieu 1991.
26. Lareau 2003.
27. Lee 2005.
28. Chiang 2009.
29. Fligstein and McAdam 2012.
30. Dezalay and Garth 1998.
31. Mansbridge and Morris 2001.
32. Polletta 1999.
33. Fanon 1967:78.
34. Muhammad 2011.
35. This passage summarizes a section of Lareau's book *Unequal Childhoods* (2003:208–217).
36. Card and Krueger 1992.
37. Bernstein 1971.
38. Hallett 2010.
39. Armstrong and Hamilton 2013.
40. Bonilla-Silva 2014:76–77.
41. Said 1978.

42. Institute for Women's Policy Research 2010.
43. For example, as recently as 2012, women accounted for only 25 percent of Fortune 500 CEOs; see Kurtzleben 2012.
44. For example, women far surpass men in terms of college completion (National Center for Education Statistics 2012).
45. West and Zimmerman 1987.
46. For a review of these theories, see Sonnert and Holton 1995.
47. Marini and Brinton 1984.
48. Kimmel 2004:237–238.
49. Hochschild 1989.
50. Udry 2000.
51. Ridgeway 2011.
52. Connell 1987.
53. Ridgeway 2014.
54. Poggi 2001.
55. Foucault [1978] 1990a:92–102.
56. See ibid., for example.
57. Sauder and Espeland 2009.
58. A. Goffman 2009.
59. Pager 2003.
60. Pettit and Western 2004.

3. STRATEGIC ACTION

1. Murphy and Welch 1989.
2. Carnevale, Strohl, and Melton 2011.
3. Ibid.
4. Ibid.
5. Homans 1958.
6. For example, a search of JSTOR, the major repository of academic journals, shows that approximately 2,075 articles discussed rational-choice theory in the past thirty years. In contrast, about 700 articles discussed Homans's social exchange theory.
7. For an extensive review of rational-choice theory, see Shepsle 2005.
8. Samuelson [1947] 1983.
9. See, for example, Becker 1976.
10. There are now rational-choice analyses of many areas of sociology. For example, Gary Becker and H. Gregg Lewis (1973) authored a

much-discussed analysis of marriage and fertility. See the subsequent discussion in the text for applications to politics and sociology.

11. Black 1948.
12. Hearn 1991.
13. Blossfeld and Shavit 1993.
14. Haller and Portes 1973.
15. Sewell, Haller, and Ohlendorf 1970.
16. Breen and Yaish 2006.
17. Jonsson 1999.
18. Coleman 1988.
19. Fukuyama 1995.
20. On ethnicity and business ownership, see, for example, Bogan and Darity 2008.
21. Small 2009.
22. Greenspan 2008.
23. Burt 1992.
24. Heaney and Rojas 2014.
25. Burt 2004.
26. Burt 1998.
27. Fligstein 2001.
28. Caro 2003.
29. Mezrich 2009.
30. Crozier 1964.
31. March and Simon 1958.
32. Cohen, March, and Olsen 1972.
33. Ibid.:2.
34. Akerlof and Kranton 2002.
35. Akerlof and Kranton 2005.
36. Ibid.
37. See Kahneman 2003 for an in-depth review of the types of biases found in this area.
38. Swidler 1986.
39. An old rational-choice joke: Two police officers see a robber rob a bank. One officer takes out a sheet of paper and starts working on some equations. The other officer says, "What are you doing? He's getting away!" The first officer says, "Don't worry, I'll catch him—he has to work out the same equilibrium!" Rim shot!
40. For an early formulation of the criticism, see Heath 1976.

41. See, for example, Gigerenzer and Engel 2006.
42. See, for example, Tilley and Holbot 2011.
43. For a review of these issues, see Sobel 2005.
44. Kingdon 2010.
45. For a clear example of the confusion and debate within the executive branch of the U.S. government about al-Qaeda, see Clarke 2004.
46. Elwert and Christakis 2006.
47. Castilla 2011; Smith 2011.

4. VALUES AND SOCIAL STRUCTURES

1. Dillon and Rotherham 2013.
2. Fitzgerald and Shah 2009.
3. Newport 2009. The Gallup poll also showed that a larger plurality didn't think NCLB made any difference at all.
4. There is a genre of popular news articles written by or about educators who complained about how NCLB changed schools. See, for example, Hobart 2008.
5. Lortie 2002.
6. See Bidwell 1965 and Johnson 1990 for structural approaches to schooling.
7. Meyer and Rowan 1977.
8. Scott and Marshall 2013.
9. People often discuss "psychological structures," the way that ideas, emotions, and memories are interrelated within the human mind. This is a fair point but not the focus of this book. I discuss only *social* structures.
10. Parsons 1937.
11. See, for example, Meyer and Rowan 1978.
12. See Alexander 1998, which includes Alexander's work from the 1980s.
13. Alexander 2004a.
14. Alexander 2004b.
15. Luhmann 1995.
16. Luhmann 1996.
17. Rojas 2013.
18. This argument is an appropriation of Kingsley Davis and Wilbert Moore's ([1945] 1970) functionalist approach to stratification.

19. For a detailed account of the minimization of standardized test scores at elite colleges, see Karabel 2005.

20. See ibid.

21. Chandler 1962.

22. Fligstein 1990.

23. Swidler 1986.

24. Ibid.:276.

25. Bellah et al. 1985:157–158.

26. Griswold 1987.

27. Joas 1997.

28. See page 24 of Swidler 2001 for Swidler's description of how she moves beyond the "culture as tool kit" argument from 1986. See pages 73–75 for the description of cultured capacities and page 87 for the passage describing cultured capacities as an "identity" theory of culture. This passage on Swidler 2001 is heavily informed by Stephen Vaisey's (2009) account of cultural sociology.

29. Parsons 1959.

30. Lawrence and Suddaby 2006.

31. Thornton and Ocasio 2008.

32. Joas 1997.

33. DiMaggio 1988.

34. Giddens 1984.

5. SOCIAL CONSTRUCTION

1. Goffman 1974.

2. See Armstrong, Hamilton, and Sweeney 2006.

3. Here, performance is very different for Goffman than it is for Jeffrey Alexander, who was discussed in chapter 4. Goffman sees all human interactions as essentially theatrical in the sense that people have roles and have to "play along" in order for the interaction to proceed. Alexander (2004a) uses performance in a much more restricted sense. When he discusses performance, he means people engaging in public displays in front of large groups of people.

4. E. Goffman [1955] 1967.

5. E. Goffman 1974.

6. Popper 2002.

7. For example, see Snow and Soule 2009:27–39.
8. See Skocpol 1979:54–55 for a discussion of this point.
9. Snow et al. 1986.
10. Ibid.
11. Heaney and Rojas 2015.
12. Rojas 2007, 2010.
13. Merton 1968:477.
14. Also see MacKenzie and Millo 2003 for an earlier formulation of this argument.
15. Bourdieu 1984.
16. Bourdieu 2001.
17. Durkheim [1893] 1997.

6. COMBINING DIFFERENT THEORIES

1. Swidler 1986.
2. Bellah et al. 1985.
3. Khan 2012.
4. It is not my purpose here to give a full definition of what the term *structuralism* means. Roughly speaking, social theory was often labeled as "structural" if the theory described how people and societies are ordered or regulated by rules. Thus, structuralist anthropology was often concerned with how preindustrial societies were organized according to kinship. Marx is considered "structuralist" because he saw societies as divided into social classes. For a more thorough history of structuralist social theory, please consult Dosse 1998.
5. For volume 1, see Foucault [1978] 1990a; for volume 2, see Foucault [1985] 1990b.
6. Foucault [1978] 1990a:92.
7. Butler 1991.
8. Tripp 2006.
9. Warner 1991.
10. See, for example, Bonilla-Silva 2014.
11. Chwe 2001.
12. See E. Goffman 1969 and Lévi-Strauss 1963; quote from Chwe 2001:96.
13. Hacking 2006.

REFERENCES

Abend, Gabriel. 2008. "The Meaning of 'Theory.'" *Sociological Theory* 26 (2):173–199.

Akerlof, George A., and Rachel E. Kranton. 2002. "Identity and Schooling: Some Lessons for the Economics of Education." *Journal of Economic Literature* 40 (4):1167–1201.

———. 2005. "Identity and the Economics of Organizations." *Journal of Economic Perspectives* 19:9–32.

Alexander, Jeffrey C. 1987. *Twenty Lectures: Sociological Theory Since World War II.* New York: Columbia University Press.

———. 1998. *Neofunctionalism and After.* Malden, Mass.: Basil Blackwell.

———. 2004a. "Cultural Pragmatics: Social Performance Between Ritual and Strategy." *Sociological Theory* 22:527–573.

———. 2004b. "From the Depths of Despair: Performance and Counter-Performance on September 11th." *Sociological Theory* 22:88–105.

Armstrong, Elizabeth, and Laura T. Hamilton. 2013. *Paying for the Party: How College Maintains Inequality.* Cambridge, Mass.: Harvard University Press.

Armstrong, Elizabeth A., Laura Hamilton, and Brian Sweeney. 2006. "Sexual Assault on Campus: A Multi-level, Integrative Approach to Party Rape." *Social Problems* 53, no. 4:483–499.

Association of American Medical Colleges. 2013. "Medical School Applicants, Enrollment Reach All-Time Highs." https://www.aamc.org/newsroom/newsreleases/358410/20131024.html. Accessed June 12, 2014.

Becker, Gary. 1976. *The Economic Approach to Human Behavior*. Chicago: University of Chicago Press.

Becker, Gary, and H. Gregg Lewis. 1973. "On the Interaction Between the Quantity and Quality of Children." *Journal of Political Economy* 81:S279–S288.

Bellah, Robert, Richard Madsen, William M. Sullivan, Ann Swidler, and Stephen M. Tipton. 1985. *Habits of the Heart: Individualism and Commitment in American Life*. Berkeley: University of California Press.

Berger, Peter L., and Thomas Luckmann. 1966. *The Social Construction of Reality: A Treatise in the Sociology of Knowledge*. Garden City, N.Y.: Anchor Books.

Bernstein, Basil. 1971. *Class, Codes, and Control*. Vol. 1: *Theoretical Studies Towards a Sociology of Language*. London: Routledge and Kegan Paul.

Bidwell, Charles. 1965. "The School as a Formal Organization." In *Handbook of Organizations*, edited by James G. March, 972–1022. Chicago: Rand McNally.

Black, Duncan. 1948. "On the Rationale of Group Decision-Making." *Journal of Political Economy* 56:23–34.

Blau, Francine D., and John W. Graham. 1990. "Black–White Differences in Wealth and Asset Composition." *Quarterly Journal of Economics* 105 (2):321–339.

Blossfeld, H-P., and Yossi Shavit. 1993. "Persisting Barriers: Changes in Educational Opportunities in Thirteen Countries." In *Persistent Inequality: Changing Educational Attainment in Thirteen Countries*, edited by Yossi Shavit and Hans-Peter Blossfeld, 1–24. Boulder: Westview Press.

Bogan, Vicki, and William Darity. 2008. "Culture and Entrepreneurship? African American and Immigrant Self-Employment in the United States." *Journal of Socio-economics* 37 (5):1999–2019.

Bonilla-Silva, Eduardo. 2014. *Racism Without Racists: Color-Blind Racism and the Persistence of Racial Inequality in America*. 4th ed. New York: Rowman & Littlefield.

Bourdieu, Pierre. 1977. *An Outline of a Theory of Practice*. Chicago: University of Chicago Press.

——. 1984. *Distinction: A Sociological Critique of Taste*. Chicago: University of Chicago Press.

——. 1990a. *Homo Academicus*. English ed. Cambridge: Polity.

——. 1990b. *The Logic of Practice*. Stanford: Stanford University Press.

———. 1991. *The Love of Art: European Art Museums and Their Public*. Stanford: Stanford University Press.

———. 1998. *State Nobility: Elite Schools in the Field of Power*. Cambridge: Polity.

———. 2001. *Masculine Domination*. Stanford: Stanford University Press.

Breen, Richard, and John Goldthorpe. 1997. "Explaining Educational Differentials." *Rationality and Society* 9:275–305.

Breen, Richard, and Meir Yaish. 2006. "Testing the Breen–Goldthorpe Model of Educational Decision Making." In *Mobility and Inequality: Frontiers of Sociology and Economics*, edited by Stephen L. Morgan, David B. Grusky, and Gary S. Fields, 232–258. Stanford: Stanford University Press.

Brennan, Geoffrey, and Loren Lomasky. 1977. *Democracy and Decision: The Pure Theory of Electoral Preference*. Cambridge: Cambridge University Press.

Burt, Ronald S. 1992. *Structural Holes: The Social Structure of Competition*. Cambridge, Mass.: Harvard University Press.

———. 1998. "The Gender of Social Capital." *Rationality and Society* 10 (1):5–46.

———. 2004. "Structural Holes and Good Ideas." *American Journal of Sociology* 110:349–399.

Butler, Judith. 1991. "Imitation and Gender Subordination." In *Inside/Out: Lesbian Theories, Gay Theories*, edited by Diane Fuss, 13–31. New York: Routledge.

Calhoun, Craig, Joseph Gerteis, James Moody, Steven Pfaff, and Indermohan Virk, eds. 2012. *Classical Sociological Theory*. New York: Wiley-Blackwell.

Caplan, Bryan. 2007. *The Myth of the Rational Voter*. Princeton: Princeton University Press.

Carby, Hazel V. 1997. "White Woman Listen! Black Feminism and the Boundaries of Sisterhood." In *Black British Feminism*, edited by Hedi Safia Mirza, 45–53. New York: Routledge.

Card, David, and Alan Krueger. 1992. "Does School Quality Matter? Returns to Education and the Characteristics of Public Schools in the United States." *Journal of Political Economy* 100 (1):1–40.

Carnevale, Anthony P., Jeff Strohl, and Michelle Melton. 2011. *What's It Worth? The Economics Value of College Majors*. Washington, D.C.: Center on Education and the Workforce, Georgetown University.

Caro, Robert. 2003. *Master of the Senate: The Years of Lyndon Johnson*. New York: Vintage.

Carson, Rachel. [1962] 2002. *Silent Spring*. Boston: Houghton-Mifflin.

Castilla, Emilio J. 2011. "Bringing Managers Back In: Managerial Influences on Workplace Inequality." *American Sociological Review* 76 (5): 667–694.

Chandler, Alfred D., Jr. 1962. *Strategy and Structure: Chapters in the History of the American Industrial Enterprise*. Cambridge, Mass.: MIT Press.

Chiang, Mark. 2009. *The Cultural Capital of Asian American Studies*. New York: New York University Press.

Chun, Jennifer Jihye, George Lipsitz, and Young Shin. 2013. "Intersectionality as a Social Movement Strategy: Asian Immigrant Women Advocates." *SIGNS* 38 (4):917–940.

Chwe, Michael. 2001. *Rational Ritual: Culture, Coordination, and Common Knowledge*. Princeton: Princeton University Press.

Clarke, Richard. 2004. *Against All Enemies: Inside America's War on Terror*. New York: Free Press.

Cohen, Michael D., James G. March, and Johan P. Olsen. 1972. "A Garbage Can Model of Organizational Choice." *Administrative Science Quarterly* 17:1–25.

Cohen-Bendahan, Celina, Cornelieke van de Beek, and Sheri A. Berenbaum. 2005. "Prenatal Sex Hormone Effects on Child and Adult Sex-Typed Behavior: Methods and Findings." *Neuroscience & Biobehavioral Reviews* 29 (2):353–384.

Coleman, James S. 1988. "Social Capital in the Creation of Human Capital." *American Journal of Sociology* 94:S95–S120.

——. 1990. *Foundations of Social Theory*. Cambridge, Mass.: Harvard University Press.

Collins, Patricia H. 1990. *Black Feminist Thought: Knowledge, Consciousness, and the Politics of Empowerment*. Boston: Unwin Hyman Press.

Collins, Randall. 1983. *Four Sociological Traditions*. Oxford: Oxford University Press.

——. 2000. *The Sociology of Philosophies: A Global Theory of Intellectual Change*. Cambridge, Mass.: Harvard University Press.

——. 2004. *Interaction Ritual Chains*. Princeton: Princeton University Press.

Connell, R. W. 1987. *Gender and Power: Society, the Person, and Sexual Politics*. Stanford: Stanford University Press.

Cook, Rebecca J., ed. 1994. *Human Rights of Women: National and International Perspectives*. Philadelphia: University of Pennsylvania Press.

Coser, Lewis. 1956. *The Functions of Social Conflict: An Examination of the Concept of Social Conflict and Its Use in Empirical Sociological Research.* Glencoe, Ill.: Free Press.

Craig, Edward. 2005. "Analytical Philosophy." In *The Shorter Routledge Encyclopedia of Philosophy*, edited by Edward Craig, 13–14. New York: Routledge.

Crozier, Michel. 1964. *The Bureaucratic Phenomenon.* Chicago: University of Chicago Press.

Dahrendorf, Ralf. 1969. *Class and Class Conflict in Modern Society.* New York: Routledge.

Davis, Kingsley, and Wilbert E. Moore. [1945] 1970. "Some Principles of Stratification." *American Sociological Review* 10:242–249.

Demeulenaere, Pierre, ed. 2011. *Analytical Sociology and Mechanisms.* Cambridge: Cambridge University Press.

Dezalay, Yves, and Bryant G. Garth. 1998. *Dealing in Virtue: International Commercial Arbitration and the Construction of a Transnational Legal Order.* Chicago: University of Chicago Press.

Dillon, Erin, and Andy Rotherham. 2013. "States' Evidence: What It Means to Make 'Adequate Yearly Progress' Under NCLB." http://www.educationsector.org/publications/states-evidence-what-it-means-make-adequate-yearly-progress-under-nclb. Accessed December 18, 2013.

DiMaggio, Paul. 1982. "Cultural Capital and School Success: The Impact of Status Culture Participation on the Grades of U.S. High School Students." *American Sociological Review* 47 (2):189–201.

——. 1988. "Interest and Agency in Institutional Theory." In *Institutional Patterns and Culture*, edited by Lynne G. Zucker, 3–22. Cambridge, Mass.: Ballinger.

DiMaggio, Paul, and Walter Powell. 1983. "The Iron Cage Revisited: Institutional Isomorphism and Collective Rationality in Organizational Fields." *American Sociological Review* 48:147–160.

Dosse, Francois. 1998. *The History of Structuralism.* Vol. 1: *The Rising Sign, 1945–1966.* Minneapolis: University of Minnesota Press.

Du Bois, W. E. B. [1935] 1992. *Black Reconstruction in America.* New York: Atheneum.

Durkheim, Émile. [1893] 1997. *The Division of Labour in Society.* Edited by L. A. Coser. New York: Free Press.

Elwert, Felix, and Nicholas A. Christakis. 2006. "Widowhood and Race." *American Sociological Review* 71 (1):16–41.

Fanon, Frantz. 1967. *The Wretched of the Earth*. Harmondsworth, U.K.: Penguin Books.

Feyerabend, Paul. 1993. *Against Method: Outline of an Anarchistic Theory of Knowledge*. New York: Verso.

Fitzgerald, John, and Paru Shah. 2009. "No Child Left Behind: The Teacher's Voice." Department of Political Science, Macalaster College. http://www.mn2020.org/assets/uploads/article/nclb.pdf. Accessed December 18, 2013.

Fligstein, Neil. 1990. *The Transformation of Corporate Control*. Cambridge, Mass.: Harvard University Press.

——. 2001. "Social Skill and the Theory of Fields." *Sociological Theory* 19:105–122.

Fligstein, Neil, and Doug McAdam. 2012. *A Theory of Fields*. Oxford: Oxford University Press.

Foucault, Michel. 1975. *Discipline and Punish: The Birth of the Prison*. New York: Pantheon Books.

——. [1978] 1990a. *The History of Sexuality*. Vol. 1: *An Introduction*. New York: Vintage Books.

——. [1985] 1990b. *The History of Sexuality*. Vol. 2: *The Use of Pleasure*. New York: Vintage.

Frazier, E. Franklin. 1997. *The Black Bourgeoisie*. New York: Free Press.

Fukuyama, Francis. 1995. *Trust: The Social Virtues and the Creation of Prosperity*. New York: Free Press.

Giddens, Anthony. 1984. *The Constitution of Society: Outline of the Theory of Structuration*. Cambridge: Polity Press.

Gigerenzer, Gerd, and Christoph Engel, eds. 2006. *Heuristics and the Law*. Cambridge, Mass.: MIT Press.

Goffman, Alice. 2009. "On the Run: Wanted Men in a Philadelphia Ghetto." *American Sociological Review* 74:339–357.

Goffman, Erving. 1959. *The Presentation of the Self in Everyday Life*. Garden City, N.Y.: Anchor Books.

——. [1955] 1967. Interaction Ritual. Garden City, N.Y.: Anchor Books.

——. 1969. *Strategic Interaction*. Philadelphia: University of Pennsylvania Press.

——. 1974. *Frame Analysis*. New York: Free Press.

Gouldner, Alvin. 1980. *The Coming Crisis of Western Sociology*. New York: Basic Books.

Granovetter, Mark. 1974. *Getting a Job: A Study of Contacts and Careers*. Cambridge, Mass.: Harvard University Press.

Greenspan, Stephen. 2008. "Fooled by Ponzi (and Madoff): How Bernard Madoff Made Off with My Money." *The Skeptic*, December 23. http://www.skeptic.com/eskeptic/08-12-23/#feature. Accessed February 28, 2014.

Griswold, Wendy. 1987. "A Methodological Framework for the Sociology of Culture." *Sociological Methodology* 17:1–35.

Gross, Neil. 2002. "Becoming a Pragmatist Philosopher: Status, Self-Concept, and Intellectual Choice." *American Sociological Review* 67:52–76.

——. 2009. "A Pragmatist Theory of Social Mechanisms." *American Sociological Review* 74:358–379.

Guo, Guang, Michael Roettger, and Tianji Cai. 2008. "The Integration of Genetic Propensities Into Social Control Models of Delinquency and Violence Among Male Youths." *American Sociological Review* 73:543–568.

Hacking, Ian. 2006. "Genetics, Biosocial Groups, and the Future of Identity." *Daedalus* 135:81–95.

Haller, Archibald O., and Alejandro Portes. 1973. "Status Attainment Processes." *Sociology of Education* 46:51–91.

Hallett, Tim. 2010. "The Myth Incarnate: Recoupling Processes, Turmoil, and Inhabited Institutions in an Urban Elementary School." *American Sociological Review* 75:152–174.

Hamilton, Peter, ed. 1991. *Talcott Parsons: Critical Assessments*. New York: Routledge.

Harlan, Louis. 1968. *Separate and Unequal: Public School and Racism in the Southern Seaboard States 1901–1915*. New York: Atheneum.

Healey, Joseph. 2011. *Race, Ethnicity, Gender, and Class: The Sociology of Group Conflict and Change*. Thousand Oaks, Calif.: Sage.

Heaney, Michael T., and Fabio Rojas. 2014. "Hybrid Activism: Social Movement Mobilization in a Multimovement Environment." *American Journal of Sociology* 119 (4):1047–1103.

——. 2015. *Party in the Street: The Antiwar Movement and the Democratic Party After 9/11*. Cambridge: Cambridge University Press.

Hearn, James C. 1991. "Academic and Nonacademic Influences on the College Destinations of 1980 High School Graduates." *Sociology of Education* 64 (3):158–171.

Heath, Anthony. 1976. *Rational Choice and Social Exchange: A Critique of Exchange Theory*. Cambridge: Cambridge University Press.

Hedström, Peter, and Richard Swedberg, eds. 1998. *Social Mechanisms: An Analytical Approach to Social Theory*. Cambridge: Cambridge University Press.

Hobart, Susan. 2008. "One Teacher's Cry: Why I Hate No Child Left Behind." *Progressive*, August 9. http://www.progressive.org/mag/hobart0808.html. Accessed December 18, 2013.

Hochschild, Arlie. 1989. *The Second Shift: Working Parents and the Revolution at Home.* New York: Viking Penguin.

Homans, George C. 1958. "Social Behavior as Exchange." *American Journal of Sociology* 63 (6):597–606.

Institute for Women's Policy Research. 2010. "Factsheet: The Gender Wage Gap: 2009." http://sarahisomcenter.org/files/2012/11/C350.pdf. Accessed December 19, 2013.

Joas, Hans. 1997. *The Creativity of Action.* Chicago: University of Chicago Press.

Johnson, Susan Moore. 1990. *Teachers at Work: Achieving Success in Our Schools.* New York: Basic Books.

Jonsson, Jan. 1999. "Explaining Sex Differences in Educational Choice: An Empirical Assessment of a Rational Choice Model." *European Sociological Review* 15:391–404.

Kahneman, Daniel. 2003. "A Perspective on Judgment and Choice: Mapping Bounded Rationality." *American Psychologist* 58:697–720.

Kahneman, Daniel, and Amos Tversky. 1979. "Prospect Theory: An Analysis of Decisions Under Risk." *Econometrica* 47 (2):263–291.

Karabel, Jerome. 2005. *The Chosen: The Hidden History of Admission and Exclusion at Harvard, Yale, and Princeton.* Boston: Houghton-Mifflin.

Khan, Shamus. 2012. *Privilege: The Making of an Adolescent Elite at St. Paul's School.* Princeton: Princeton University Press.

Kimmel, Michael. 2004. *The Gendered Society.* Oxford: Oxford University Press.

Kingdon, John. 2010. *Agendas, Alternatives, and Public Policies.* 2nd ed. New York: Pearson.

Knapp, Steven, and Walter Benn Michaels. 1982. "Against Theory." *Critical Inquiry* 8 (4):723–742.

Kuhn, Thomas S. 1962. *The Structure of Scientific Revolutions.* Chicago: University of Chicago Press.

Kurtzleben, Danielle. 2012. "Women Make Little Progress Atop Fortune 500 in 2012." *US News & World Report*, December 19. http://www.usnews.com/news/articles/2012/12/19/women-make-little-progress-atop-fortune-500-in-2012. Accessed August 12, 2016.

Lareau, Annette. 2003. *Unequal Childhoods: Class, Race, and Family Life*. Berkeley: University of California Press.

Lawrence, Tom, and Roy Suddaby. 2006. "Institutions and Institutional Work." In *The Sage Handbook of Organization Studies*, edited by Stewart R. Clegg, Cynthia Hardy, Thomas B. Lawrence, and Walter R. Nord, 215–254. London: Sage.

Lee, David. 2005. *The Battle of the Five Spot: Ornette Coleman and the New York Jazz Field*. Oklahoma City: Mercury Press.

Lemert, Charles, ed. 2010. *Social Theory: The Multicultural and Classic Readings*. Philadelphia: Westview Press.

Levine, Donald K. 1995. *Visions of the Sociological Tradition*. Chicago: University of Chicago Press.

Lévi-Strauss, Claude. 1963. *Structural Anthropology*. Translated by Claire Jacobson and Brooke Grundfest Schoepf. New York: Basic Books.

Lin, Nan. 2002. *Social Capital: A Theory of Social Structure and Action*. Cambridge: Cambridge University Press.

Loewen, James. 2005. *Sundown Towns: A Hidden Dimension of American Racism*. New York: New Press.

Lortie, Dan C. 2002. *Schoolteacher: A Sociological Study*. Chicago: University of Chicago Press.

Lounsbury, Michael, and Ed Carberry. 2005. "From King to Court Jester? Weber's Fall from Grace in Organizational Theory." *Organization Studies* 26:501–525.

Luhmann, Niklas. 1995. *Social Systems*. Stanford: Stanford University Press.

——. 1996. *The Reality of the Mass Media*. Stanford: Stanford University Press.

Lukes, Steven. 1974. *Power: A Radical View*. New York: Macmillan.

MacKenzie, Donald. 2006. *An Engine, Not a Camera: How Financial Models Shape the Markets*. Cambridge, Mass.: MIT Press.

Mackenzie, Donald, and Yuval Millo. 2003. "Negotiating a Market, Performing Theory: The Historical Sociology of a Financial Derivatives Exchange." *American Journal of Sociology* 109:107–145.

Mansbridge, Jane, and Aldon Morris, eds. 2001. *Oppositional Consciousness: The Subjective Roots of Social Protest*. Chicago: University of Chicago Press.

March, James, and Herb Simon. 1958. *Organizations*. New York: Wiley-Blackwell.

McCarthy, John D., and Mayer N. Zald. 1977. "Resource Mobilization and Social Movements: A Partial Theory." *American Journal of Sociology* 82 (6):1212–1241.

Merton, Robert K. 1968. *Social Theory and Social Structure*. New York: Free Press.

Meyer, John W., and Brian Rowan. 1977. "Institutionalized Organizations: Formal Structure as Myth and Ceremony." *American Journal of Sociology* 83:340–363.

——. 1978. "The Structure of Educational Organizations." In Marshall W. Meyer and associates, *Organizations and Environments*, 78–109. San Francisco: Jossey Bass.

Mezrich, Ben. 2009. *The Accidental Billionaires: The Founding of Facebook. A Tale of Sex, Money, Genius, and Betrayal*. New York: Doubleday.

Mises, Ludwig von. 1949. *Human Action: A Treatise on Economics*. New Haven: Yale University Press.

Mooney, Margaret Marini, and Mary Brinton. 1984. "Sex Typing in Occupational Socialization." In *Sex Segregation in the Workplace: Trends, Explanations, Remedies*, edited by Barbara Reskin, 192–232. Washington, D.C.: National Academy Press.

Muhammad, Khalil. 2011. *The Condemnation of Blackness: Race, Crime, and the Making of Modern Urban America*. Cambridge, Mass.: Harvard University Press.

Mullings, Leith, and Alaka Wali. 2000. *Stress and Resilience: The Social Context of Reproduction in Harlem*. New York: Kluwer Academic Press.

Murphy, Kevin, and Finis Welch. 1989. "Wage Premiums for College Graduates: Recent Growth and Possible Explanations." *Educational Researcher* 18 (4):17–26.

National Center for Education Statistics. 2012. "Table 234: Recent High School Completers and Their Enrollment in 2-Year and 4-Year Colleges, by Sex: 1960 Through 2011." *Digest of Education Statistics*. http://nces.ed.gov/programs/digest/d12/tables/dt12_234.asp. Accessed August 12, 2016.

Nelson, Alondra. 2016. *The Social Life of DNA: Race, Reparations, and Reconciliation After the Genome*. Boston: Beacon Press.

Newport, Frank. 2009. "Americans Doubt Effectiveness of 'No Child Left Behind.'" Gallup, August 19. http://www.gallup.com/poll/122375/americans-doubt-effectiveness-no-child-left-behind.aspx. Accessed June 12, 2014.

Pager, Devah. 2003. "The Mark of a Criminal Record." *American Journal of Sociology* 108 (5):937–975.

Park, Robert, and Ernest Burgess. 1921. *Introduction to the Science of Sociology*. Chicago: University of Chicago Press.

Parsons, Talcott. 1937. *The Structure of Social Action*. Glencoe, Ill.: Free Press.

——. 1951. *The Social System*. Glencoe, Ill.: Free Press.

——. 1959. "The School Class as a Social System: Some of Its Functions in American Society." *Harvard Educational Review* 49:298–318.

——. 1977. *The Evolution of Societies*. Upper Saddle River, N.J.: Prentice-Hall.

Parsons, Talcott, Edward Shils, Kaspar Naegele, and Jesse R. Pitts, eds. 1965. *Theories of Society: Foundations of Modern Sociological Theory*. Glencoe, Ill.: Free Press.

Pettit, Becky, and Bruce Western. 2004. "Mass Imprisonment and the Life Course: Race and Class Inequality in U.S. Incarceration." *American Sociological Review* 69 (2):151–169.

Phillips, Bernard. 2001. *Beyond Sociology's Tower of Babel: Reconstructing the Scientific Method*. Piscataway, N.J.: de Gruyter.

Piven, Frances Fox, and Richard A. Cloward. 1971. *Regulating the Poor: The Functions of Social Welfare*. New York: Vintage.

Poggi, Gianfranco. 2001. *Forms of Power*. Cambridge: Polity Press.

Polletta, Francesa. 1999. "Free Spaces in Collective Action." *Theory and Society* 28:1–38.

Popper, Karl. 2002. *The Logic of Scientific Discovery*. New York: Routledge.

Portes, Alejandro. 1998. "Social Capital: Its Origins and Applications in Sociology." *Annual Review of Sociology* 24:1–24.

Ridgeway, Cecilia. 2011. *Framed by Gender: How Gender Inequality Persists in the Modern World*. Oxford: Oxford University Press.

——. 2014. "Why Status Matters for Inequality." *American Sociological Review* 79 (1):1–16.

Ritzer, George. 2008. *Sociological Theory*. New York: McGraw-Hill.

Roemer, John. Ed. 1986. *Analytical Marxism*. Cambridge: Cambridge University Press.

Rojas, Fabio. 2007. *From Black Power to Black Studies: How a Radical Social Movement Became an Academic Discipline*. Baltimore: Johns Hopkins University Press.

——. 2010. "Power Through Institutional Work: Building Academic Authority in the 1968 Third World Strike." *Academy of Management Journal* 53:1263–1280.

——. 2013. "Institutions." In *Oxford Bibliographies in Sociology*, edited by Jeff Manza. Oxford: Oxford University Press. http://www.oxfordbibliographies .com/view/document/obo-9780199756384/obo-9780199756384-0132 .xml?rskey=zRg207&result=44&q=. Accessed August 12, 2016.

Rubin, Gayle. 1975. "The Traffic in Women: Notes on the 'Political Economy' of Sex." In *Toward an Anthropology of Women*, edited by Rayna Reiter, 157–210. New York: Monthly Review Press.

Said, Edward W. 1978. *Orientalism*. New York: Vintage Books.

Samuelson, Paul. [1947] 1983. *Foundations of Economic Analysis*. Cambridge, Mass.: Harvard University Press.

Sassen, Saskia. 1991. *The Global City: New York, London, Tokyo*. Princeton: Princeton University Press.

Sauder, Michael, and Wendy Espeland. 2009. "The Discipline of Rankings: Tight Coupling and Organizational Change." *American Sociological Review* 74:63–82.

Scott, John, and Gordon Marshall. 2013. "Structure." In *A Dictionary of Sociology*, edited by John Scott and Gordon Marshall. Oxford: Oxford University Press. http://www.oxfordreference.com/view/10.1093/acref /9780199533008.001.0001/acref-9780199533008. Accessed August 12, 2016.

Searle, John. 1997. *The Construction of Social Reality*. New York: Free Press.

Selznick, Phil. 1961. "The Social Theories of Talcott Parsons." *American Sociological Review* 26:932–935.

Sewell, William H., Archibald O. Haller, and George W. Ohlendorf. 1970. "The Educational and Early Occupational and Status Attainment Process: Replication and Revision." *American Sociological Review* 35 (6):1014–1027.

Shepsle, Ken. 2005. *Rational Choice Institutionalism*. Cambridge, Mass.: Harvard University Press.

Simmel, Georg. 1972. *Georg Simmel on Individuality and Social Forms*. Edited by Donald K. Levine. Chicago: University of Chicago Press.

Skocpol, Theda. 1979. *States and Social Revolutions: A Comparative Analysis of Russia and China*. Cambridge: Cambridge University Press.

Small, Mario L. 2009. *Unanticipated Gains: Origins of Network Inequality in Everyday Life*. New York: Oxford University Press.

Smith, E. B. 2011. "Identities as Lenses: How Organizational Identity Affects Audiences' Evaluation of Organizational Performance." *Administrative Science Quarterly* 56 (1):61–94.

Snow, David A., R. Burke Rochford Jr., Steven K. Worden, and Robert D. Benford. 1986. "Frame Alignment Processes, Micromobilization, and Movement Participation." *American Sociological Review* 51:464–481.

Snow, David, and Sarah Soule. 2009. *A Primer on Social Movements*. New York: Norton.

Sobel, Joel. 2005. "Interdependent Preferences and Reciprocity." *Journal of Economic Literature* 43:392–436.

Sonnert, Gerhard, and Gerald Holton. 1995. *Gender Differences in Science Careers: The Project Access Study*. New Brunswick, N.J.: Rutgers University Press.

Swidler, Ann. 1986. "Culture in Action: Symbols and Strategies," *American Sociological Review* 51:273–286.

——. 2001. *Talk of Love: How Culture Matters*. Chicago: University of Chicago Press.

Tavory, Iddo, and Stefan Timmermans. 2014. *Abductive Analysis: Theorizing Qualitative Research*. Chicago: University of Chicago Press.

Terriquez, Veronica. 2015. "Intersectional Mobilization, Social Movement Spillover, and Queer Youth Leadership in the Immigrant Rights Movement." *Social Problems* 62:1–20.

Thornton, Patricia H., and William Ocasio. 2008. "Institutional Logics." In *Handbook of Organizational Institutionalism*, edited by Royston Greenwood, Christine Oliver, Kerstin Sahlin, and Roy Suddaby, 99–129. Thousand Oaks, Calif.: Sage.

Tilley, James, and Sara B. Holbot. 2011. "Is the Government to Blame? An Experimental Test of How Partisanship Shapes Perceptions of Performance and Responsibility." *Journal of Politics* 73 (2):316–330.

Tilly, Charles. 1978. *From Mobilization to Revolution*. Boston: Addison-Wesley.

Tolnay, Stewart E., Glenn Deane, and E. M. Beck. 1996. "Vicarious Violence: Spatial Effects on Southern Lynchings, 1890–1919." *American Journal of Sociology* 102:788–815.

Tripp, Clarence Arthur. 2006. *The Intimate World of Abraham Lincoln*. New York: Basic Books.

Udry, Richard J. 2000. "Biological Limits of Gender Construction." *American Sociological Review* 65 (3):443–457.

U.S. Census Bureau. 2012. *The 2012 Statistical Abstract of the United States*. Washington, D.C.: U.S. Census Bureau.

Vaisey, Stephen. 2009. "Motivation and Justification: A Dual-Process Model of Culture in Action." *American Journal of Sociology* 114 (6):1675–1715.

Wallerstein, Immanuel. 1979. *The Capitalist World-Economy*. Cambridge: Cambridge University Press.

Wall Street Journal. 2012. Law-School Enrollment and Degrees Awarded. July 30. http://online.wsj.com/news/articles/SB10000872396390444860104577 558914050201888. Accessed June 12, 2014.

Warner, Michael. 1991. "Introduction: Fear of a Queer Planet." *Social Text* 9 (4):3–17.

Weber, Max. [1905] 1958. *The Protestant Ethic and Spirit of Capitalism*. Translated by Talcott Parsons. New York: Scribner's.

——. 2010. "Ethnic Segregation and Caste." In *Social Theory: Multicultural and Classic Readings*, 4th ed., edited by Charles Lemert, 124–126. Boulder: Westview Press.

West, Candace, and Don H. Zimmerman. 1987. "Doing Gender." *Gender & Society* 1 (2):125–151.

Williams, D. R., and S. A. Mohammed. 2009. "Discrimination and Racial Disparities in Health: Evidence and Needed Research." *Journal of Behavioral Medicine* 32:20–47.

Willis, Paul. 1981. *Learning to Labor: How Working Class Kids Get Working Class Jobs*. New York: Columbia University Press.

Woodson, Carter Godwin. 1990. *The Mis-education of the Negro*. Trenton, N.J: Africa World Press.

INDEX

GPSR Authorized Representative: Easy Access System Europe, Mustamäe tee
50, 10621 Tallinn, Estonia, gpsr.requests@easproject.com

www.ingramcontent.com/pod-product-compliance
Lightning Source LLC
Chambersburg PA
CBHW032134020426
42334CB00016B/1159